SECOND SUPPLEMENT

TO

THE FIRST EDITION

OF THE

HISTORY

OF

BRITISH FISHES,

BY

THE LATE WILLIAM YARRELL, V.P.L.S., F.Z.S.

BEING ALSO A FIRST SUPPLEMENT TO THE SECOND EDITION.

ILLUSTRATED WITH WOODCUTS.

EDITED BY SIR JOHN RICHARDSON, C.B.

LONDON:
JOHN VAN VOORST, PATERNOSTER ROW.
M.DCCC.LX.

In the interest of creating a more extensive selection of rare historical book reprints, we have chosen to reproduce this title even though it may possibly have occasional imperfections such as missing and blurred pages, missing text, poor pictures, markings, dark backgrounds and other reproduction issues beyond our control. Because this work is culturally important, we have made it available as a part of our commitment to protecting, preserving and promoting the world's literature. Thank you for your understanding.

PREFACE

TO THE

SUPPLEMENT TO THE SECOND EDITION.

THIS Supplement is published for the use of the purchasers of Mr. Yarrell's First and Second editions of his History of British Fishes, and contains all the species that have been discovered in the British Seas since the year 1839, as far as they have come to the knowledge of the Editor.

Lancrigg, Grasmere, 1859.

NAMES OF FISHES IN THIS SUPPLEMENT.

FIRST VOLUME.

			Place in First Edition.	Second Edition.
Fabricius' Sea-Bullhead	. After page	69	84
Couch's Sea-Bream	,,	103	119
The Bogue	,,	116	132
The Dotted Mackerel	,,	133	150
The Germon	,,	142	159
The Pelamid	,,	142	159
The Derbio	,,	142	159
Bank's Oar-fish	,,	190	223

SECOND VOLUME.

The Sail-fluke	. After page	250	341
The Connemara Sucker	,,	279	376
The Common Sturgeon	,,	359	474
The Gray Notidanus	,,	386	517
The Petromyzon Juræ	,,	472	628

A

HISTORY

OF

BRITISH FISHES.

BY

WILLIAM YARRELL, F.L.S., V.P.Z.S.

VOL. III.—SUPPLEMENTARY.

LONDON:
JOHN VAN VOORST, PATERNOSTER ROW.
M.DCCC.LX.

MEMOIR OF WILLIAM YARRELL.

WILLIAM YARRELL was a man rather below the middle height, having a robust, well-knit frame, a sagacious and pleasing countenance, and frank and agreeable manners. His aspect was that of a stout yeoman, such as those who in times past have contributed with head and hand to elevate their native England to its present rank among the nations; or rather his demeanour may be said to have indicated exactly what he was in fact—a citizen who had thriven in the greatest of commercial cities, but who, strong in native honesty and self-respect, had passed unscathed through the perils of money-making, his cheerful countenance bearing no lines traced by the thirst of gain or the debasing passion for hoarding: on the contrary, his mild but fearless eye, and his open forehead, showed, even to a stranger, a man at peace with himself and with his fellow men.

He was born on the 3rd of June, 1784, in the parish of St. James's, where his home continued to be for the seventy-two years of his life. In Duke Street his father and uncle carried on in partnership the business of newspaper agents. On the death of his father, his mother removed to a private residence in Great Ryder

MEMOIR OF WILLIAM YARRELL.

Street, and there the son lived with her, and during that time was joined in trade with his cousin, then carrying on the business of their late fathers at the north-east corner of Little Ryder Street, to which house it had been removed; and whither, on Edward Jones ceasing to reside, William Yarrell went, and continued to dwell, till death.* A domicile so permanent offers no field for stirring incident, but it is salutary to contemplate the career of a man, who, possessing the ability, judgment and industry that lead to success, and placed by the accidents of birth and connection among the busy throng of the metropolitan worshippers of wealth, deliberately chose the safer middle path of competency,—in an age when money has power to raise its possessor to a seat among the law-givers of the land, and the art of acquiring it is considered in the social estimate of the day as equivalent to high breeding, education and virtue, —when, in short, the cry " get money, *per fas aut nefas*," has gone far towards sapping the national character for honesty, and the vaunted good faith of the British merchant is in danger of becoming a myth.

The following brief narrative is compiled from obituary notices published immediately after Mr. Yarrell's death by several of his intimate and attached friends— Professor Bell, President of the Linnean Society, Dr. R. G. Latham, Edward Newman and Lovell Reeve, Esqs. These gentlemen have referred mainly to Mr. Yarrell's scientific pursuits, and have mentioned few or no particulars of his private life, nor is the compiler of this memoir able to supply the deficiency. But he, who attained the length of days usually allotted to man, and survived all his brothers and sisters as well as father and

---

* A year before that event, he had ceased to have any connection with the business, having retired in favour of Messrs. Joseph and Charles Clifford.

MEMOIR OF WILLIAM YARRELL. vii

mother, though he never married, must have had the depths of his sensitive nature often stirred by the breaches made by death in the circle of his relatives and friends, even should no tenderer tie have been untimely snapt asunder. That such was the case may be inferred from the feeling which only two years before his death prompted him to transfer to the album of his relatives, the Misses Pallett of Dover, the subjoined lines from Wordsworth :—

> " first and last,
> The earliest summoned and the longest spared,
> Are here deposited."

The following is the marriage certificate of his parents :—

" At Bermondsey Parish Church, Surrey, Francis Yerrall, of this Parish, Bachelor, to Sarah Blane, of this Parish, Spinster. By Banns, 26 June, 1772.

Present, William Hawkins,
John Beszant."

Subsequently his father transposed the e and a in writing his surname, as appears by this register of birth :—

" St. James's, Westminster, June 27, 1784. William Yarrell, son of Francis and Sarah, born June 3rd."

Of his father's origin, except that he was born the 10th of February, 1749, married the 26th of June, 1772, died the 25th of March, 1794, was the eldest of seven brothers and sisters, the children of Francis Yerrall, born in 1727, died the 5th of January, 1786, and of Sarah his wife, born in 1719, died the 12th of December, 1800,—nothing can now be ascertained ; and it is believed that the son never knew his father's native place exactly, though he used to think that he came from Bedfordshire, where the surname is a common one, but is spelt in various ways. The second Francis Yerrall is reported to have been a proud man. Sarah Blane is said by a relative to have been born of parents who were small farmers at Bayford in Herts, and to have been remarkable for nothing but a tartness of temper, wholly unlike to that of her distinguished son. If the dispositions of the mind are, as has been supposed, like the constitution of the body and the lineaments of the countenance, in some degree hereditary, and that consequently pride and quickness of temper descended to the offspring of Francis and Sarah Yarrell, William, the ninth-born child, was fortunately endowed at the same time with so much firmness and good sense as to be able to keep his passions under control and to become remarkable in after-life for modesty and urbanity.

In his boyhood William Yarrell occasionally visited his maternal relatives at Claypits Farm, Bayford, and there, doubtless, his love of rural scenery originated; but his earliest tastes for Natural History seem to have been fostered by his mother, who took him with her in the frequent excursions she made to Margate, then a favourite resort of Londoners. Their conveyance was the usual one of the time, the Margate Hoy, and young Yarrell found amusement on the sands in picking up sea-weeds, which he and his sister afterwards laid out on paper. He also collected shells and other marine productions.

His school days were passed at the large scholastic establishment kept by Dr. Nicholas at Ealing, where he acquired the character of a quiet, studious boy. The late General Sale, G. S. Heales, Esq., of Doctors' Commons, who survived him but a few months, and Mr. Edward Jones, were his fellow pupils, the last-mentioned

MEMOIR OF WILLIAM YARRELL.

being his cousin, the son of his father's partner, and his own future associate in the business carried on in Ryder Street. He had also for playmates his relatives, Mr. Bird and Mr. Goldsmith.

In 1802, being then in the eighteenth year of his age, he entered the banking-house of Herries, Farquhar and Co., as a clerk, but shortly afterwards left that employ, and returned to his father's business. Previous to this event his love of angling had made him acquainted with the streams in the vicinity of London, and the perusal of Izaac Walton's fascinating colloquies had taught him to combine practical philosophy with that pastime. In the course of this pursuit he afterwards often associated with a Londoner of maturer years, an old sportsman named Adams, with whom he was wont to angle under Putney bridge and in other parts of the Thames when the calls of business did not press. Under the guidance of this early friend he acquired the art of shooting, and as it was his custom throughout life to pursue zealously whatever he undertook, he became a proficient in the management of the gun. This led to an intimacy with George Manton, the well-known gun-maker of Bond Street, and with Shoobridge, the hatter of Bond Street, known among sporting men as an unerring shot. Yarrell, who was thought by some to be the better shot of the two, became a member of the Old Hats Club, and was a successful competitor at shooting matches near London. He was constantly in friendly consultation with George Manton when any new form of breech or lock in a fowling-piece was to be tried. At a later time he shot game in Hertfordshire and Cambridgeshire over different manors which he rented in conjunction with his friend Wortham. His exploits with the gun are still remembered in the neighbourhood of Royston, and the

MEMOIR OF WILLIAM YARRELL.

same healthful exercise led him also frequently into other localities. His tastes, says one of his friends, were those of a Londoner, whom the *rus in urbe* suited better, perhaps, than the unmixed country. They were those of Izaac Walton, citizen and angler, rather than those of the full and perfect yeoman.

These amusements of his earlier life led to his acquiring an intimate knowledge of the habits of our native birds and fishes, their food and migrations, his observation of the objects that engaged his attention being as accurate as it was keen. They were not, however, the only occupations in which he sought relief from the monotony of business, for in 1817 he studied Chemistry at the Royal Institution. Before he attained middle life he engaged in the systematic study of Zoology, and pursuing it in the intervals of business with his accustomed application, he gradually gave up field sports, and it is believed that for thirty years before his death he handled neither rod nor gun.

In 1823 he commenced noting the appearance of strange and rare birds, and in 1825 he lent his aid to Bewick by sending him scarce British birds to figure. He also presented a collection of the tracheæ of water-birds to the Royal College of Surgeons. His own museum at this time contained a series of British Birds and their eggs, and he now cultivated the society of scientific men, among whom he had made the acquaintance of Sir William Jardine, Bart., and P. J. Selby, Esq., of Twizel House, who were then engaged in publishing their respective works on British Ornithology. In November of the same year he was admitted a Fellow of the Linnean Society, and in 1826 he became one of the original members or founders of the Zoological Society. Next year he was chosen to be one of the

MEMOIR OF WILLIAM YARRELL.

Council of the Medico-Botanical Society, and henceforward his readiness to oblige, the clearness of his understanding, and his business habits, coming to be known, his services in the management of the societies to which he belonged were in constant requisition. " It was only with reluctance, and in compliance with established rules," says Professor Bell, " that his name was omitted from the council lists of either the Linnean or Zoological Societies." Of the latter he was occasionally Auditor, for a time Secretary, and frequently one of its Vice-Presidents. He was also a warm supporter, and for a long time treasurer, of the Entomological Society. On the death of Mr. Forster, in 1849, he was elected Treasurer of the Linnean Society, and continued to fill that office and to be one of its Vice-Presidents until his death. With respect to the Royal Society, the following is the statement of Professor Bell, who was fully cognizant of the circumstances : " Many years since, long before the present plan of selecting a certain number of candidates by the Council was adopted, Mr. Yarrell was proposed as a Fellow, and his certificate signed and suspended. At that time the Council had nothing whatever to do with the election nor with the recommendation of the candidates. Mr. Yarrell's scientific character was not so well known and appreciated as it has since become. A gentleman, long since deceased, who would afterwards have gladly recalled the act, expressed some objection to his being elected, and his certificate was, from a feeling of delicacy on Mr. Yarrell's part, withdrawn ; but subsequently, since the present system has been in action, the writer of this notice, with the full concurrence of many members of the Council, who were most desirous of his election, drew up a certificate in his favour, and obtained some signatures before he mentioned the subject to Mr. Yarrell, hoping that when he knew such a step had been taken he would consent to be put in nomination. On being informed, however, of this movement, which there is no doubt would have met with the unanimous approval of the Council, he declined the honour solely on the ground of advancing age, and his increasing inability to avail himself of the advantages of the position."

The subjoined list of Mr. Yarrell's publications affords evidence of his industry and the variety of his zoological studies. He became an author evidently from the love of his subjects, and being in no haste to publish until he had duly investigated the matter in hand and brought his clear judgment to bear on the evidence before him, his writings on Natural History soon acquired that value among scientific men which simple and truthful narrative always commands. His great works on the Birds and Fishes of Britain are quoted as authorities in all the scientific circles of Europe and America, and are models of local Faunæ, both on account of the strictness with which doubtful species are noted or rejected, as well as for the completeness of the lists gained by unwearied diligence and inquiry in every direction. The synonymy is elaborated with care and skill, and the illustrations, liberally provided by his friend and publisher, are worthy of the works, which is no mean praise. Mr. Yarrell and Mr. Van Voorst were first brought together by their mutual friend, the late Mr. Martin, the librarian of the Duke of Bedford, and the conjunction was a most fortunate one for the progress of British Zoology, a series of unrivalled illustrated monographs having originated therefrom. Mr. Yarrell's inquiries into the changes of plumage of hen Pheasants and of birds generally, his dissertations on the horny tip of the bill of young chickens,

MEMOIR OF WILLIAM YARRELL.

on the production and migration of Eels, on the gestation of eggs by the male Pipe-fish, his investigations into the route pursued by American birds in their casual visits to England, and numerous other passages of his works, show much originality of thought and a careful examination of facts.

One of his friends * says, " There was one trait in the character of Mr. Yarrell which must not be passed over in silence, a trait which no one was better acquainted with than myself, and that was his extreme readiness to afford information. Often have I had occasion to appeal to him in difficulties about specific character or points of economy, and from the very moment of mentioning the doubt or the object of inquiry, his whole attention was absorbed by it ; books, specimens, memory, every auxiliary was at his finger-ends ; and no sacrifice of time or trouble was too great for him to make ; neither was the subject ever left undecided while diligence or a disposition to teach could throw on it a single ray of light. No other subject seemed to occur to him during the investigation ; he had no other occupation ; that one inquiry was, for the time, the object of his life. His power of concentrating his attention on a single subject was most extraordinary, and more extraordinary still was the facility with which that concentrated attention was turned to *any* subject; he used it after the fashion of a burning glass, casting the focus wherever he pleased. This faculty was at the service of all ; and the attention of which I speak thus gratefully from personal experience was given to every truth-seeking inquirer."—*Zoologist,* 5258.

Another friend † writes as follows : " Mr. Yarrell's

---

* Edward Newman, Esq., Editor of the Zoologist.

† Dr. R. G. Latham.

xiv MEMOIR OF WILLIAM YARRELL.

purely intellectual character is seen in his works. The part which the author himself always took most credit for, was the geographical distribution of birds. He considered that in treating it as he had done, he smuggled in a certain amount of geography under the garb of ornithology. For the high qualities of accuracy, terseness of description, and felicity of illustration, they speak for themselves."—*Edinburgh New Philosophical Journal,* 1856.

So much for the excellence of his works on Zoology, of which the best tests are the continually-increasing demand for them at home after twenty-two years' circulation, and the frequency and confidence with which they are quoted by naturalists abroad. With regard to Mr. Yarrell's character as a man, the following extracts from the obituary notices referred to, will show the estimation in which he was held by those who were most intimately acquainted with his conduct in private and public life. "Strong social instincts," says a keen observer of men and manners, "geniality of temper, warmth of heart (exhibited in an extreme fondness for children), made him loved, even as his simple and straightforward independence of character made him respected. His advice, too, was always valued, freely asked and freely given, for his mind was observant, active, practical, and wholly unclouded by fancies or prejudices; his knowledge varied and accurate. Indeed he was essentially a reliable man, knowing what he knew well, and caring to undertake nothing that he was likely to fail in. For this a strong will and perseverance is needed. It was strong enough to keep a warm temper in thorough control; for Mr. Yarrell, knowing what was due to himself, knew also what was due to others. He helped many, not only with his advice but by his purse, ever valuing money for

MEMOIR OF WILLIAM YARRELL.

its uses only, never for its own sake; moderate (as a man of business) in his aims, though attentive to what he undertook; hating waste, yet never ambitious of accumulation." . . . . " For many years his house was familiar to all naturalists, and to visitors of every rank from the country, not to mention foreigners, to whom the reputation of one of the soundest of living zoologists was well known, aud who never visited it without being struck by the kind and communicative manners of its hospitable inmate." . . . . " His habits, angler and ornithologist as he was, were eminently those of a Londoner. He loved glees, and sung them well, and at one time of his life was a frequent attendant at the theatres."—*Dr. R. G. Latham.*

The testimony of Professor Bell, who knew him well, is as follows:—" In speaking of Mr. Yarrell's intellectual and social qualities, it is difficult to do them justice without danger of appearing hyperbolical. His judgment was clear and sound, his appreciation of the value of facts and of evidence most accurate, his advice always practical and thoughtful. His truthfulness and simpleheartedness were even child-like, his temper gentle, his heart loving and affectionate, and he was liberal and charitable almost to the verge of imprudence. A kindlier spirit never lived. His friendships were sincere and lasting, and only changeable on discovery of the worthlessness of the subject, and then how hard was he to believe the painful truth! If ever man realized the beautiful apostolical definitions of Charity, it was William Yarrell. There were, indeed, in Mr. Yarrell's character many points of resemblance to that of Izaac Walton and of Gilbert White. The same charming *bonhomie* and truthfulness and simplicity and elegant taste as in the former; and the close and accurate obser-

xvi MEMOIR OF WILLIAM YARRELL.

vation and clear and graphic description which characterize the writings of the latter."

A third friend (Mr. Lovell Reeve) mentions the following traits of character :—" Notwithstanding his retired manners, Mr. Yarrell was a frequent diner-out, and a jovial companion at table. He sang a capital song, and was a constant attendant at the theatre, generally selecting, with the gusto of a dilettante, the front row of the pit. In the days of the elder Mathews, he would manage to get the songs of the great mimic, in spite of the rapidity of their utterance, by taking down the alternate lines one night, and filling in the others on the next. A song of Dibdin's we heard him sing only recently, with admirable spirit and pathos. He seldom missed the Linnean Club dinners and country excursions, and was at all times the liveliest of the party."

By the methodical distribution of his time Mr. Yarrell was enabled, without neglecting his business concerns, to assist in the management of the scientific societies of which he was a member, and to carry on his zoological inquiries and publications. His enjoyment of social life was combined with temperance; and being blessed with a sound constitution he possessed continuous good health up to the year 1853, when some premonitory symptoms of indisposition began to appear, without, however, affecting the activity of his intellect or the cheerfulness of his manners. On the 3rd of August, 1856, as he was returning from St. James's Church, which for some years he had constantly attended, a slight giddiness seized him, his steps became uncertain, and he felt for a moment unable to proceed. After a short rest he reached home without assistance. This attack proved to be a slight paralysis, from which

MEMOIR OF WILLIAM YARRELL.

he so far recovered as to able to give his uninterrupted attention to matters of business. On Monday, the 25th of August, he attended a Council of the Linnean Society, and was as cheerful, and apparently nearly as well as usual. In answer to a wish expressed by his intimate and attached friend the President of the Society, that he would soon be able to pay him a quiet visit, he said that though pretty well he felt a "wooliness" in the brain, and that he was restricted in his diet. On the following Saturday, however, he felt himself well enough to take charge of an invalid friend in a voyage by sea to Yarmouth, and thus the very last act of his life was one of kindness. He enjoyed the voyage, took a moderate dinner at the Royal Hotel with appetite, and retired to bed anticipating a good night's rest. But scarcely had he lain down before he felt a difficulty of breathing, and fearing, as he said, that "he might die and no one know it," he got up, unlocked the door, and rang the bell. The attentive landlady was speedily at his bedside, medical assistance was procured without delay, but nothing availed, and he expired calmly at half-past twelve on Monday morning the 1st of September, in the seventy-third year of his age. He experienced no pain, and remained perfectly conscious until within a few minutes of his entering the unseen world. The immediate cause of his death was judged to be disease of the heart, with which the previous symptoms of apoplexy were but indirectly connected. No autopsy was made. On the following Monday he was buried at Bayford in Hertfordshire (where a great many of his maternal kinsfolk and ancestors lie), in a spot selected by himself, his body being attended to the grave by the President and other office-bearers of the Linnean Society, as well as by his executors and surviving relatives.

xviii   MEMOIR OF WILLIAM YARRELL.

A tombstone erected to his memory bears the following inscription :—

HERE LIE THE REMAINS

OF

WILLIAM YARRELL, V.P.L.S., F.Z.S.,

of St. James's, Westminster,

Author of a History of British Birds, and of a History of British Fishes.

BORN, JUNE 3rd, MDCCLXXXIV.
DIED, SEPT. 1st, MDCCCLVI.

He was the survivor of twelve Brothers and Sisters, who, with their Father and Mother, are placed close to this spot.

" first and last,
The earliest summoned and the longest spared—
Are here deposited."—WORDSWORTH.

His executors were his relative Mr. Bird, and his friend and publisher Mr. Van Voorst, and the property administered to amounted to about 17,000l. After his death his extensive library of Natural History books and his valuable collections of British Birds and Fishes were sold by auction, at which the Fishes were purchased for the British Museum.

A portrait of him, painted in 1839 by Mrs. Carpenter, is suspended in the hall of Burlington House, the expense having been defrayed by forty Fellows of the Linnean Society ; and a Medallion Tablet executed by Mr. Neville Burnard, has been affixed in St. James's Church, at the west end of the north aisle.

The portrait facing the title-page of Vol. I., engraved by Mr. Frederick A. Heath, is from a photograph by Messrs. Maull and Polyblank, taken in 1855.

LIST OF MR. YARRELL'S WRITINGS.

1. Notices of the occurrence of some rare British Birds observed during the years 1823, 1824, and 1825.—*Zool. Journ.*, ii. p. 24, March, 1825.

2. Ditto, second communication.—*Zool. Journ.*, iii. p. 85, October, 1826.

3. Ditto, third communication.—*Zool. Journ.*, iii. p. 497.

4. Some observations on the anatomy of the British Birds of Prey.—*Zool. Journ.*, iii. p. 181, October, 1826.

5. On the small horny appendage to the upper mandible in very young chickens.—*Zool. Journ.*, ii. p. 443, written 17th October, 1825, published 1826.

6. Notice of the occurrence of a species of duck (*Anas rufina*) new to the British Fauna.—*Zool. Journ.*, ii. p. 492, 1826.

7. Observations on the tracheæ of Birds, with descriptions and representations of several not hitherto figured.—*Linn. Trans.*, xv. p. 378, 1827. Read February 6th, 1827.

8. On the change of plumage of some Hen Pheasants.—*Phil. Trans.*, written February, 1827. Read in May, 1827.

9. On the osteology of the Fennec (*Canis cerdo*).—*Zool. Journ.*, iii. p. 401, 1827.

10. On the osteology of the *Chlamyphorus truncatus* of Dr. Harlan, March, 1828.—*Zool. Journ.*, iii. p. 544.

11. Some remarks on the habits of the Kingfisher, March, 1828.—*Loudon's Mag. of Nat. Hist. and Journ. of Zool., &c.*, i. p. 23, 1828.

12. Description of a species of Tringa (*T. rufescens*) killed in Cambridgeshire, new to England and Europe.—*Linn. Trans.*, xvi. p. 109. Read June 17th, 1828.

13. On the supposed identity of Whitebait and Shad, August, 1828.—*Zool. Journ.*, iv. p. 137.

LIST OF MR. YARRELL'S WRITINGS.

14. Observations on the Tapir of America. — *Zool. Journ.*, iv. p. 210.

15. On the use of the Xiphoid bone and its muscles in the Cormorant (*Pelecanus carbo*, L.), August, 1828.—*Zool. Journ.*, iv. p. 234.

16. Notes on the internal appearance of several animals examined after death, in the collection of the Zoological Society (Otter, Paradoxure, Ocelot, Chinchilla, Agouti, Porpoise, Touraco, Javanese Peacock, Silver Pheasant, Hybrid Pheasant, White Stork, Common Bittern, Crested Grebe, Red-throated Diver, Tame Swan, Wild Swan, Black Swan, Canada Goose, White-fronted Goose, Indian Tortoise, Active Gibbon, Diana Monkey, Weeper Monkey, Mexican Dog, Jerboa, Bobac, Malabar Squirrel, Crested Porcupine, Alpine Hare).—*Zool. Journ.*, iv. pp. 314-322.

17. On the structure of the beak and its muscles in the Cross-bill (*Loxia curvirostra*).—*Zool. Journ.*, iv. p. 459.

18. Remarks on some English Fishes, with notices of three species new to the British Fauna (*Solea pegusa, Cottus bubalis, Anguilla*).—*Zool. Journ.*, iv. p. 465.

19. Descriptive and Historical Notice of British Snipes.—*Loudon's Mag. of Nat. Hist., &c.*, ii. p. 143, 1829.

20. Supplement to ditto.—*Loudon's Mag. of Nat. Hist.*, iii. p. 27, 1830.

21. On the organs of voice in Birds.—*Linn. Trans.*, xvi. p. 305. Read June, 1829.

22. On a new species of Wild Swan (*Cygnus Bewickii*) taken in England, and hitherto confounded with the Hooper.—*Linn. Trans.*, xvi. p. 445. Read January, 1830.

23. Reply to the statement respecting the Discovery of *Cygnus Bewickii*, published in the Philosophical Magazine and Annals for August.—*Richard Taylor's Philos. Mag. and Annals.*

24. On the occurrence of the *Sylvia Tithys* of Scopoli in England.—*Proceed. of Com. of Science of Zool. Soc.*, i. p. 18, 1830.

25. On the assumption of the male plumage by the female of the common Game Fowl.—*Ibid.*, i. p. 22, 1830.

26. On the anatomy of the *Cereopsis Novæ Hollandiæ*, Lath., and on the relations between the *Natatores* and *Grallatores.—Ibid.*, i. p. 25, 1830.

27. On the sexual organs of the hybrid Pheasant.—*Ibid.*, i. p. 27.

28. On the specific identity of the Gardenian and Night Herons (*Ardea Gardenii* and *nycticorax*).—*Ibid.*, i. p. 27.

29. On the Anatomy of the *Chinchilla lanigera.—Ibid.*, i. p. 32.

29*. On the trachea of the Red-knobbed Curassow (*Crax Yarrellii*, Benn.).—*Ibid.*, i. p. 33.

LIST OF MR. YARRELL'S WRITINGS. xxi

30. Characters of a new species of Herring (*Clupea*, L.).—*Ibid.*, i. p. 34.

31. On the occurrence of several North American Birds in England.—*Ibid.*, i. p. 35.

32. On the anatomy of the Lesser American Flying Squirrel (*Pteromys volucella*).—*Ibid.*, i. p. 38.

33. On the anatomy of the *Ctenodactylus Massonii*, Gray.—*Ibid.*, i. p. 48.

34. On the sterno-tracheal muscles of the Razor-billed Curassow (*Ourax mitu*, Cuv.).—*Ibid.*, i. p. 59.

35. On the distinctive characters of the *Tetrao medius*, Temm.—*Ibid.*, i. p. 73.

36. On two species of Entozoa in the Eel.—*Ibid.*, i. p. 132.

37. On the generation of Eels and Lampreys.—*Ibid.*, i. p. 132.

38. On the Brown-headed Gull (*Larus capistratus*, Temm.).—*Ibid.*, i. p. 151.

39. On the anatomy of the Conger Eel (*Conger vulgaris*), and on the differences between the Conger and the Fresh-water Eels.—*Ibid.*, i. p. 159.

40. Additions to the British Fauna, Class Fishes, September, 1830.—*Loudon's Mag. of Nat. Hist.*, iii. p. 521.

41. Specific characters of *Cygnus Bewickii* and *C. ferus.*—*Taylor's Phil. Mag. and Annals*, vii. p. 194.

42. Additions to the catalogue of British Birds, with notices of the occurrence of several rare species, January, 1831.—*Loudon's Mag. of Nat. Hist.*, iv. p. 116.

43. On a hybrid between a Muscovy Duck (*Anas moschata*) and a Common Duck (*Anas boschas*).—*Proc. Com. of Sc. of Zool. Soc.*, ii. p. 100, 1832.

44. On two species of Mammalia new to Britain, one of them (*Sorex remifer*) new to science.—*Ibid.*, ii. p. 429, 1832.

45. Description of the organs of voice in a new species of Wild Swan (*Cygnus buccinator* of Richardson).—*Linn. Trans.*, xvii. p. 1. Read 20th March, 1832.

46. Description of three British species of Fresh-water Fishes belonging to the genus *Leuciscus* of Klein.—*Ibid.*, xvii. p. 5. Read June, 1832.

47. Additions to the British Fauna, Class Mammalia (*Arvicola riparia, Sorex remifer*), August, 1832.—*Loudon's Mag. of Nat. Hist.*, v. p. 598.

48. Notice of a new species of Herring.—*Zool. Journ.*, v. p. 277.

49. Observations on the laws which appear to influence the assumption and changes of plumage in Birds.—*Proceed. Zool. Soc.*,

VOL. I.   (*2nd Supp.*)   c

xxii LIST OF MR. YARRELL'S WRITINGS.

i. pp. 9, 56; *Trans. Zool. Soc.*, i. p. 13. Read February and April, 1833.

50. Description, with some additional particulars, of *Apteryx australis* of Shaw.—*Proc. Zool. Soc.*, i. p. 24; *Trans. Zool. Soc.*, i. p. 71. Read June, 1833.

.51. On the trachea of the *Penelope gouan*, Temm., and the *Anas magellanica*, Auct.—*Proceed. Zool. Soc.*, i. p. 3.

52. On the Woolly and Hairy Penguins (*Aptenodytes*).—*Proceed. Zool. Soc.*, i. pp. 24, 80; *Trans. Zool. Soc.*, i. p. 13, 1833.

53. On the identity of the Woolly Penguin of Latham with the *Aptenodytes patachonica* of Gmelin.—*Proceed. Zool. Soc.*, i. p. 33, 1833.

54. Characters of the Irish Hare, a new species of *Lepus*.—*Ibid.*, i. p. 88.

55. On the deficiency of teeth in the hairless Egyptian variety of the dog.—*Ibid.*, i. p. 113.

56. Notice of the occurrence of *Squilla Desmarestii* on the British shores.—*Loudon's Mag. of Nat. Hist., &c.*, vi. p. 230.

57. On the reproduction of the Eel.—*Report of Brit. Assoc.*, 1833, p. 446.

58. On the anal pouch of the male fishes in certain species of *Syngnathus.*—*Proceed. Zool. Soc.*, ii. p. 118.

59. Observations on the economy of an insect destructive to turnips (*Athalia centifolia*).—*Trans. Zool. Soc.*, ii. p. 67. Read November, 1835.

60. On the mode of union after fracture of the processes of the vertebræ of a Sole (*Solea vulgaris*, Cuv.).—*Proceed. Zool. Soc.*, iii. p. 57, 1835.

61. On the trachea of the Stanley Crane (*Anthropoides paradiseus*, Besch.).—*Ibid.*, iii. p. 183.

62. On the fœtal pouch of the male Needle Pipe-fish (*Syngnathus acus*, L.).—*Ibid.*, iii. p. 183, 1835.

63. A History of British Fishes. Van Voorst, London, 1836, 2 vols., 8vo., (published in parts, finished in 1836, containing vol. i. pp. 408, vol. ii. pp. 472).

64. Supplement to ditto, March, 1839 (vol. i. pp. 48, vol. ii. pp. 78, containing 27 new species).

64*. On an interwoven mass of filaments of *Conferva fluviatilis* of extraordinary size.—*Proceed. Linn. Soc.*, i. p. 65, 1838.

65. A History of British Fishes. Van Voorst, London, 1841, 2 vols., 8vo., Second Edition (vol. i. pp. 464; vol. ii. pp. 628, containing 263 species, and 500 figures).

66. A History of British Birds. Van Voorst, London, 1843, 3

LIST OF MR. YARRELL'S WRITINGS. xxiii

vols., 8vo. (published in parts at intervals of two months, the first one in July, 1837, and the last one in May, 1843. Vol. i. pp. 525; vol. ii. pp. 669; vol. iii. pp. 528).

67. Supplement to ditto, October, 1845 (number of species in the first edition and supplement 354).

68. A History of British Birds. Van Voorst, London, 1845, 3 vols., 8vo., Second Edition.

69. On a new species of Swan (*Cygnus immutabilis*).—*Proceed. Zool. Soc.*, ix. p. 70, 1841.

70. On the trachea of a male Spur-winged Goose (*Anser gambensis*).—*Ibid.*, ix. p. 70, 1841.

71. On a new species of Smelt from the isle of Bute (*Osmerus hebridicus*).—*Report of Brit. Assoc. for* 1838, p. 108.

72. On the preservation of *Crustacea.*—*Entom. Mag.*, vi. p. 421.

73. Remarks on some species of *Syngnathus.*—*Annals of Nat. Hist. and Mag. of Zool., Jardine, &c.*, iii. p. 81.

74. Growth of Salmon in fresh water.—*Ibid.*, iv. p. 334.

75. On *Motacilla alba*, L.—*Ibid.*, vii. p. 350.

76. Description of the eggs of some of the birds of Chile.—*Zool. Proceed.*, 1847.

77. Occurrence of a Petrel new to Britain on the coast of Ireland, June, 1853.—*Zoologist*, 3947.

78. On birds lately ascertained to be British, p. 79; and on rare English fishes, p. 85.—*Ibid.*, 79. 1843.

79. On the influence of the sexual organ in modifying external character.—*Journ. Linn. Soc.*, June, 1856, i. p. 76.

80. On Mucor observed by Colonel Montagu in the air-cells of a bird.—*Annals and Mag. of Nat. Hist., &c.*, ix. p. 131.

81. Chapter VIII. in the Third Edition of Harvey's Sea-side Book "On Marine Fishes," pp. 237-269.

SECOND SUPPLEMENT
TO THE FIRST VOLUME OF
THE HISTORY OF BRITISH FISHES.

ACANTHOPTERI.   *SCLEROGENIDÆ.*

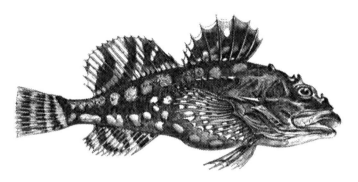

FABRICIUS'S SEA-BULLHEAD.

KANIOK, *Greenland Eskimos.*

Acanthocottus groenlandicus, GIRARD.
Cottus scorpius, FABRICIUS, F. Groenl. p. 156 (excl. syn.).
,, *groenlandicus,* CUV. et. VALENC. Poiss. vol. iv. p. 185.
,,   ,,   RICHARDSON, F. Bor. Am. iii. pp. 46, 297, 314, pl. 95.
,,   ,,   *Greenl. Bullhead,* THOMPS. Nat. Hist. of Irel. iii. p. 81.

AN example of this species was captured in Dingle Harbour in February 1850, and exhibited in the Dublin Natural History Society, by Mr. William Andrews. As yet, this and one seen by Dr. Ball, are the only recorded examples of the fish that have been met with on our shores. The figure at the head of the article, which corresponds closely with the one published by Mr. Andrews, and the vignette at the end, are borrowed from the *Fauna Boreali Americana,* where a Newfoundland specimen is described at length.

This, Fabricius says, is a most voracious fish, and very

SCLEROGENIDÆ.

destructive of the fry of Blennies, Salmon, Herrings, and Haddocks. It even attacks larger fish, does not spare its own species, devours crabs and worms, and in fact pursues every living thing that it can master.* It is bold, lively, and incautious; but habitually keeps at the bottom of the sea, coming to the surface only when it is led thither in pursuit of its prey. It spawns in December and January, depositing its roe on sea-weeds. It is prized as an article of food by the Greenland Eskimos, who eat it daily both boiled and dried, and find it agreeable and wholesome for the sick. Many of them eat its eggs raw; and some even consume the fish itself in that condition. They capture it with lines armed with four hooks, disposed crosswise, and with no other bait than something coloured or shining placed above the hooks. Sometimes they spear it.

The female, Fabricius states, is larger than a male of the same age, and may be distinguished at once by its white belly, which appears yellow in the water and is spotted. The posterior cranial tubercles are nearer to each other in the males than in the females. There are four of these tubercles on the upper aspect of the head, one at each corner of an area, which in the female is nearly square and flat. There are besides eight spines on each half of the head and shoulders, viz. a nasal, opercular, subopercular, scapular, and humeral one, with three preopercular ones. The principal spine is the one at the angle of the preoperculum. Its tip falls about its own length short of the point of the opercular spine. The interval between the orbits is much depressed, and

---

* The omnivorous appetite ascribed to this Bullhead by Fabricius was proved by an examination of the contents of the stomachs of several Newfoundland specimens, which consisted of the vertebral columns of several small fishes, some entire crabs, the peelings of potatoes, and other substances. These Bullheads were caught off the end of a landing jetty.

THE SEA-BULLHEAD.

is bounded anteriorly by the two nasal spines and the prominent ends of the premaxillary pedicles. There are no serratures on any of the spines or bones of the head or shoulder, in which respects this species differs from the Father-Lasher.

The top of the head is sprinkled with soft conical pimples, and the skin generally is naked and smooth, but some small, circular, minutely-spiniferous scales exist on the back and posterior surfaces of the pectoral rays.

Br. 6: D. 10—17 or 18: A. 12 or 13: P. 17: V. 1+3: C. 11¾.

Colours, after the specimen had been kept in spirits, dark brown on the dorsal aspect, mixed with clay-coloured patches on the head, and crimson blotches on the gill-covers, nape and pectorals. The sides, belly, pectoral fins, and ventrals, are ornamented with circular spots of dead white, each surrounded by a dark rim. The liver has a bright red colour in the spirits.

FRONT OF COTTUS GROENLANDICUS.

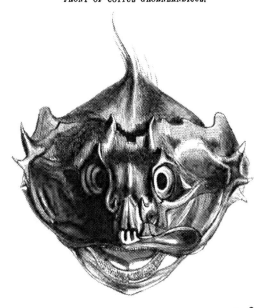

ACANTHOPTERI.

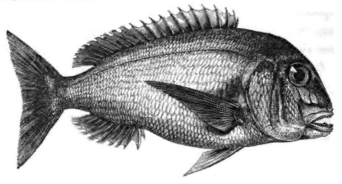

COUCH'S SEA-BREAM.

Pagrus orphus, Le Pagre Orphe, Cuv. et Valenc. vi. p. 150, pl. 149.
"*Aurata orphus*"   ,,   ,,   Risso, 2ᵉ edit. p. 356.
Couch's Sea-Bream,   ,,   Couch. (Ion.) Zool. for 1843, p. 81.
Pagellus Rondeletii,   ,,   Couch. (B.Q.) Zool. for 1846, p. 1406.

ONLY one example of this fish is known to have been captured on the English coast, and, as is the case with several other occasional or rare visitants of the Cornish shores, we owe its enrolment in the list of British Fishes to the acuteness and active zeal of Jonathan Couch, Esq. The specimen figured above was taken on the 8th of November 1842 with a baited hook, at a rocky place termed the Edges, three miles south of Polperro. Its weight was six pounds. Mr. Couch having presented the specimen to the British Museum, Dr. Gray, Keeper of the Zoological Department of that Institution, has most kindly furnished the following account of it:—

"The specimen is stuffed. The front teeth above and below are four on each side, the upper ones being conical, the lower ones elongato-conical, and set widely apart. Behind these, but in the front part of both jaws, there is a crowded patch of small subulate teeth. On the limbs of the jaws the molars are large with globular crowns, and rounded teeth of unequal size cover the roof of the mouth. The fish is moderately like fig. 149, in the *Histoire des Poissons*, but that figure does not show space enough between the tall conical teeth in front of the mandible, and the flat molars on the limb of the bone. The specimen also has a higher front than the figure referred to, with more resemblance in profile to *Pagellus calamus*, fig. 152, of the same work. This elevation of the face may be owing to age, for the specimen figured in the *Histoire des Poissons* was only eight inches long, while the one in the British Museum measures above twenty. (For a side view of the mouth see p. 36.)

D. 12+11 : A. 3+9 : V. 1+5 : P. 15 : C. 29.

The last two rays of the dorsal and anal are contiguous at the base, and the last ventral ray is also divided to the bottom." — *Gray*.

Mr. Couch says, that the body is not unlike the *Pagellus centrodontus*, but is rather deeper and more stout. The head is thick, and the snout remarkably so. The back rises high above the head. The colour of the front and top of the head was a brownish-red, that of the back and fins between lake and vermilion, or like the Becker, except the anal, which was pale-yellow: the sides being pale-red and the belly whitish.—*Couch*.

TEETH OF COUCH'S SEA-BREAM.

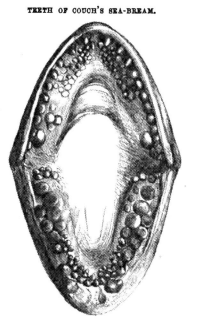

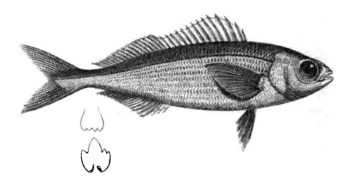

THE BOGUE.

BOGA, *Provence, Madeira.*—BOBBA, *Venice.*—UOPPA, *Messina.*—BALAIJOLA, *Catania.*

Box vulgaris, Le Bogue commun,	CUVIER et VALENC. vi. p. 348, pl. 161.
Box vel Boops,	,, ,,	BELON. de Aq. p. 230.
,, ,, ,,	,, ,,	RONDELET, Pisc. p. 136.
Boops Rondeletii primus,		WILLUGHBY, 317, t. U. 8. f. 1.
Box vulgaris, Common Bogue,		YARRELL, Zool. for 1843, p. 85.

Box or Boops. *Generic Character.*—Body elongated, rounded, the dorsal and ventral profiles alike, and the general aspect peculiarly trim. Mouth small; premaxillary very little movable, overlapped together with the maxillary and edge of the mandible by the preorbitar when the mouth is shut. Teeth uniserial, incisorial, chisel-shaped, lobed, and crenated. Stomach very small, with a long pyloric branch, and about five pancreatic cæca. Air-bladder large, thin, and nacry, with two long, posterior, horn-like appendages, which enter among the muscles of the tail.

THE BOGUE, or BOGA, abounds in the Mediterranean, and as it has an Atlantic range southwards to Madeira and the Canaries, and according to Cornide, northwards to the coasts of Galicia, it is precisely one of the fish that might be expected to pay occasional visits to the southern extremity of England, but Alfred Fox, Esq., of Falmouth, is the only person who as yet has had the fortune

THE BOGUE.

to recognise and secure an English example of the species. That specimen was caught at St. Mawes, in a ground seine, early in October 1843, and deposited by Mr. Fox in the Museum at Truro, where it is preserved, stuffed, and varnished. Through the kindness of Dr. Barham, Senior Physician of the Cornwall Infirmary, the specimen has been lent that the subjoined description might be taken of it, but the figure on the preceding page is copied from one in the *Histoire des Poissons*, which was drawn from a fresh specimen, rather than from the Truro one, which has suffered mutilation in the fin-rays.

The genera *Box, Oblata, Boxaodon* (Guich.), *Scatharus*, and *Crenidens*, form the fourth Sparoid tribe of Cuvier, and are characterized by simple, lobed or serrated, trenchant teeth set closely side by side on the edges of the jaws; sometimes with villiform teeth behind them, or more often with many-crowded rows of minute teeth having a villiform appearance to the naked eye, but being in fact similar in form to the large incisorial ones that constitute the exterior row, and destined to succeed them as they wear away and drop out. In this tribe there are no rounded molars on the limbs of the jaws, which, consequently, are neither so strong nor so thick as in the members of the first tribe, which have broad molars, that necessarily require space. In accordance with the dentition the mouth of *Box* and its allies is small, and the neat head is very unlike that of the bull-headed *Chrysophrydes* and *Pagri*.

The Bogue, according to the *Histoire des Poissons*, spawns twice in the year, and at these times it approaches the shore in large sculls. The fishermen of Provence and Nice take it in nets of a peculiar kind, named by them *bughiera*, and to render the fishery more prosperous, they adorn their boats with small figures of the Bogue cut

8 SPARIDÆ.

in silver. Rondelet says that the flesh of the Bogue is
easily digested, and on that account is a wholesome ali-
ment for invalids, but Cornide, who speaks of it as he
observed it on the Atlantic coasts of Spain, states that it
has a disagreeable taste, and is consumed chiefly by poor
people. Mr. Lowe tells us that it is exceedingly common
at Madeira, and though he says nothing of its qualities
as an article of food, he remarks of another species of the
same genus that it is one of the handsomest and most
worthless of fishes.

The Bogue has an elegant, moderately-compressed, elliptical form, the curves of the dorsal and ventral profiles
meeting at the terminal mouth which is slightly obtuse.
The greatest height of the body is at the fifth or sixth
dorsal spinous ray, and is contained thrice and one-half
times in the length, excluding the caudal fin. The head
makes a fourth of the same distance, or a fifth of the entire
length of the fish, including the caudal fin. The face forms
part of the general dorsal curve without inequalities, and
the crown of the head is moderately rounded transversely,
the width at the posterior angles of the orbits being a
little more than a diameter of the eye, but at the anterior
angles a little less. The nostrils are small pore-like open-
ings in a membrane near the anterior angle of the orbit,
and close to the upper end of the preorbitar.

The mouth is very small, and is armed above and below with a single close-set series of incisorial teeth,
which are channelled in front, bevelled and crenated on
the edges. The minute crenatures of each of the upper
teeth number about seven or eight, the cutting edges being otherwise nearly straight; but the lower teeth have
a convexly-curved edge, and from the depth of the
lateral crenatures are more or less lobed; in the St.
Mawes specimen none of the under teeth have the

THE BOGUE. 9

strongly-projecting middle lobe represented in the *Histoire des Poissons;* and if it existed in the younger fish, it has worn down in the older specimen before us. Cuvier enumerates twenty-four teeth in the upper jaw, but the jaws being only half open in the example we are describing, we cannot reckon beyond nine or ten on each premaxillary or limb of the mandible.

The preorbitar is highest anteriorly, and narrows gradually towards its termination under the centre of the pupil, its length being about twice its greatest height; the rest of the suborbitar chain is narrow, the whole forming a half circle close beneath the eye, with a silvery lustre and many pores. The mandible has the same kind of porous nacry surface on its under aspect, and all the naked parts of the head seem to be copiously mucigenous. The upper edges of the mandible, as far back as the articulation of the jaw, are received under the preorbitars, which also wholly cover the maxillaries and all the lateral portions of the premaxillaries. A crescentic band of scales, five deep in the centre of the crescent, covers the cheek entirely between the suborbitar chain and the naked preopercular disk, which has a perfectly even hyperbolically-curved edge.

Four rows of smaller scales cover the interoperculum, which, when the jaws are closed, touches its fellow, and conceals the branchiostegous membrane. The posterior margin of the gill-cover is a small segment of a circle, of which the suboperculum constitutes about two-thirds. A small shallow obtuse notch, with rounded corners, terminates the bony edge of the operculum, above the level of the pectoral fin: with the lower corner of the notch the point of the suboperculum coincides exactly so that there is no projection, and neither bone nor notch would be perceptible in a recent specimen. The membranous edge of the gill-cover is very narrow, and the disk is covered with six rows of scales nearly as large as those on the body, but diminishing to five and four rows as they descend over the suboperculum whose junction with the operculum they wholly conceal. From opposite the upper corner of the opercular notch, a strip of scaleless very porous integument curves upwards and forwards to the mesial line of the occiput opposite the posterior angles of the orbits where it meets its fellow: it includes the porous disk of the suprascapula, which looks like a scale, and is bounded posteriorly by eight or nine scales, being the commencement of those on the body, but appearing larger from their whole disks being exposed. On the temples between the naked border of the orbit and the humero-nuchal arc of integument, there is a short isolated patch of scales ranged in four rows. With this exception, the top of the head, the snout, and jaws are destitute of scales.

The lateral line bounds the upper fourth part of the height, having a rather flatter curve than the back: it is composed of seventy-eight scales, exclusive of the small scales on the base of the caudal, where the line cannot be traced in the dried specimen. Where the body is highest there are six rows of scales above the row which forms the lateral line, and about twelve below, all ranged so as to form nearly a semicircular curve between the dorsal and ventral profiles, and having a Sciænoid aspect, with more or less obliquity. The free border has a smooth nacry surface, with many little pits, producing the same appearance of frosted silver which the naked parts of the head exhibit. A detached scale has a straight base, impressed with six, eight, ten, or more furrows, separated by ridges that diverge, like the rays of a fan, from a point situated in the posterior third of the disk: the sides are also straight, and the free margin is curved, and smooth when its nacry epidermis is entire; but the adjoining half of the disk is composed of microscopical polygonal areas, like denticles worn down, and the exterior row of these denticulate the margin when the epidermis is removed: the lines of structure run parallel to the free edge and sides, bending at the angles to do so.

(D. 14+15: A. 3+16: P. 18: V. 1+5: C. 15⅔.—(*Hist. des Poiss.*)

The coloured drawing of the British specimen sent by Mr. Fox to Mr. Yarrell is not among the papers handed to the Editor of the present edition of British Fishes, but the following tints are enumerated by Cuvier, who describes a fresh specimen. "The back is yellowish-olive, and the belly silvery. Three or four bright golden lines traverse the sides." Even in the dried specimen the course of these lines can be traced.

The total length of the specimen is about ten inches.

MULL OF CANTYRE.

The barrier of that iron shore.—SCOTT.

THE DOTTED MACKEREL.

Scomber punctatus, Couch, Zool. 1849, p. xxix. App. fig.
,,   ,,   Id. Rep. to Penz. Nat. Hist. Soc. for 1848, pl. iii. f. 1.
,,   ,,   White, Cat. Brit. Mus. p. 30.

This fish was taken in a Mackerel Seine at Looe, in Cornwall, on the 6th of July, 1848, and fortunately fell into the hands of Jonathan Couch, Esq., the able and industrious cultivator of Cornish ichthylogy. As no second example has as yet been met with, and the chief peculiarities of the Dotted Mackerel are its colours and markings, its specific rank may remain a question, until the acquisition of other specimens furnish the means of investigating its internal structure. In the meanwhile Mr. Couch's description is quoted from the Zoologist. The figure is from a drawing by him.

"The length of the specimen was fifteen inches and a half, and the general proportions were those of the Common Mackerel. Conspicuous scales, marked by minute transverse lines, cover the sides and belly, where none are distinguishable in the common species. There was no corselet, but there was some appearance of it in a line of denser scales above the pectoral fin which vanished below that fin. The dorsals were three inches apart.

D. 12—11, V: P. 20.

"The tail at the setting on of the caudal fin is depressed and square. Lateral line waved. The colour afforded a marked distinction from the Common Mackerel, being of an uniform dark neutral tint, or bluish-olive, green on the head and back without any coloured bands or variations, but with green reflections on the sides: round, well-defined spots, of the size of a small pea, cover the sides thickly from head to tail; on the summit of the back they are a little larger, and are transversely elongated; they end a little below the lateral line, the belly being pure white. Between the caudal crests the surface is a bronzed yellow. The specimen was a female, and had an air-bladder."—*Couch, l. c.*

WHEEL AND SPINDLE, ST. ANDREW'S.

"Prima diocœsis et antiquissima regni
Patroni Andreæ nobile nomen habet."
(*Carmen de Fifa*, SIBBALD.)

"St. Rule, a monk of Patræ, in Achaia, warned by a vision, A.D. 370, is said to have sailed westward till he landed at St. Andrew's, where he founded a chapel and tower."—SCOTT, *Marmion*, i. *notes.*

ACANTHOPTERI.

THE GERMON.

Thynnus alalonga, Le Germon, Cuvier et Valenc. viii. p. 120, t. 215.
Germon, Barbot, Churchill's Voy. v. pl. 29 (1732).
Alilonghi, Duhamel, Peches, pp. 203, 207.
Ala-longa, Cetti, Hist. Nat. Sard. iii. p. 191.
Orcynus alalonga, Couch (Jon.), MSS. fig.
Long-finned Tunny, Couch (R. Q.), Zool. 1413, with fig.

Cuvier considers it to be one of the most remarkable facts in the history of ichthyology, that this fish of great size, very distinct in its characters, excellent as an article of food, and the subject of productive fisheries on the coasts of Europe, should have remained unnoticed by ichthyologists until a recent period. Though it is captured in abundance on the north coasts of Spain, facing the Bay of Biscay, and appears to be not uncommon on the French Atlantic coasts as high as Rochelle, it either rarely enters the English Channel, or it has been overlooked by British naturalists as much as it had been by those of Spain and France. It is to the Messieurs Couch, father and son, that we owe its introduction into the list of English fishes. Mr. R. Q. Couch informs us in the Zoologist for 1846 that two

THE GERMON. 15

specimens have been taken in Mount's Bay by fishermen who have spread their seines for Mackerel. One of them in the year 1846, whereof the published figure is quoted above, and the other, which was captured several years previously, was then deposited in the Penzance Museum of Natural History.

This fish ought to interest Englishmen peculiarly, since its appellation of *Germon*, by which it was first made known to science, is supposed to be a corruption of the word War-man, in use at the Ile d'Yeu, when the English were masters of Guienne and Poitou. The Basques name it *hegalalonchia*, which signifies long-winged, and the French mariners also, with reference to the length of its pectorals, call it *long-oreille* (long-ear). Cuvier had not the means of comparing Mediterranean with Atlantic specimens of this fish ; their identity, therefore, rests on the accuracy of the details given in books. His description was drawn up from a specimen procured from Rochelle, and ought to accord with the British fish.

M. Noel de la Moriniere has given the best account of the fisheries of the Germon on the French Atlantic coasts. The fishermen of Ile d'Yeu begin the fishery in the south of the Bay of Biscay opposite St. Sebastians, follow the fish in their movements to the north of Belleisle; and the numbers they capture in a season average 13,000 or 14,000. They use lines of eighty fathoms in length, and bait their hooks with salted eel, but the Germon being very voracious, a piece of white or blue cloth or some shining piece of earthenware, or tin cut into the form of a Pilchard, often serves the purpose.

The Germons arrive in the Bay of Biscay in numerous bands about the middle of June, sometimes a few come as early as May, and they continue to be met with as

16 SCOMBRIDÆ.

late as October. Their fishery is generally two months later than that of the Tunny. The Germons prey on Mullets, Pilchards, Anchovies, and other fishes that assemble in sculls, and they also pursue the Flying-fishes. When the Germons come to the surface of the water, the fishermen take few, and large captures are only made at great depths. Experience alone points out the places where they may be sought with success, and when once the fishermen fall in with a scull of these fish, they pursue it till the end of the season. A cloudy sky, a fresh north-west or south-west wind, and a gently-agitated sea, are favourable for this fishery. When in full season, that is, in July and August, the meat of the Germon is whiter and more delicate than that of the Tunny, and fetches a better price, but before and after these months it is inferior. These details are borrowed from the *Histoire des Poissons*, wherein the history of the species is carried to a much greater length.

The specimen described in the Zoologist by Mr. R. Q. Couch was eighteen inches long and five high, excluding the vertical fins. The Germon has the usual form of the Tunnies, and a thickness equal to about two-thirds of its height. The falcate pectoral reaches as far towards the tail as the middle of the anal fin. The corselet, composed of larger scales, commencing on the humeral chain, embraces the base of the pectoral, and extending as far as that fin reaches, forms a recess in which the fin lies when it is laid to the side of the fish. The formula for the fin-rays is—

P. 37 : D. 14—3+12, VIII. : A. 3+12, VIII. : V. 1+5 : C. 40.

There are three graduated spines buried in the front of the soft dorsal and anal, and eight detached finlets follow each of these fins. The ventrals are closely approxi-

THE GERMON. 17

mated to each other, and between them there is a slender scale which looks like an additional ray. The caudal fin is widely crescentic with very short rays towards the middle. The mouth is small, and the mandible is longer than the upper jaw. The teeth are small, and not thickly set on the jaws. On the palatines and tongue they are very short and densely villiform. The colour of the specimen was blackish-blue or deep mackerel tint on the dorsal aspect, fading on the ventral surface into pale blue, yellow, and white. These particulars are chiefly from Mr. Couch.

THE TUMMEL AT BONSKIED.

ACANTHOPTERI.   SCOMBRIDÆ.

THE PELAMID.

Pelamys sarda, La Pélamide,   Cuv. et Val. t. viii. p. 149, tab. 217.
  ,,   *vera Aristotelis,*   Rondelet, 238.   a.d. 1554.
Pelamis,   Salvian, 123.   a.d. 1554.
Thunnus,   Aldrovand, 213.   a.d. 1640.
Pelamys Belloni,   Willughby, 180.   a.d. 1686.
Scomber ponticus,   Pallas, Zoogr. vol. iii. p. 217.   a.d. 1831.
  ,,   ,,   Bloch, 334.
Pelamys sarda, La Pélamide,   Webb et Berth. Can. Poiss. p. 50.
Scomber sarda, Bonetta,   Mitchill, New York Trans. vol. i. p. 428, No. 8.

Pelamys. *Generic Characters.*—The general shape of the members of this group is fusiform, and they have a cutaneous keel on each side of the slender part of the tail. On the coracoidal or pectoral region, scales of larger size form a corselet; elsewhere the scales are small and tender, passing, on the belly, into soft nacry integument. The dorsals are contiguous; and the first one has its rays, which are spinous, connected by a continuous membrane: behind the second dorsal there are numerous detached finlets, and one or two fewer behind the anal. The branchiostegals are seven. These, and other characters, they have in common with the Tunnies (*Thynni*); but they are distinguished by having longer and stronger subulate teeth on the jaws, widely set. The head is conical, with a rather fine apex formed by the symphyses of the equally long jaws.

This fine fish has a wide distribution, having been taken of full size on the Russian coasts of the Black Sea, in all districts of the Mediterranean, and on both sides of the Atlantic—on the east side from the Cape Verds and Canaries, northwards along the coast of Spain,

THE PELAMID. 19

and on the west side off Connecticut, at New York, and on the Brazil coast. Ichthyologists might naturally have looked in the British seas for this active and wide-travelling fish, especially on the Cornish or Irish coasts; but the first of our naturalists who has had the fortune to procure a British example, or at least to recognise the species, is William Beattie, Esq., Honorary Secretary of the Montrose Natural History and Antiquarian Society. The specimen was captured in a salmon-net set at the mouth of the North Esk, which falls into the North Sea in latitude $56\frac{3}{4}°$, and fortunately came into the possession of a gentleman competent to understand the value ichthyologists set on such a discovery. Before intelligence of this fish reached us the entire impression of the third edition of British Fishes had been printed off; but as there had been no issue, we are enabled to interpolate this notice in the place that the species ought to occupy in the volume: and we beg to tender many thanks to Mr. Beattie and Dr. Gray for their communications; and to the directors of the Montrose Society for their liberality in lending the specimen.

According to Pallas, the Black Sea specimens attain the length of an ell; Webb and Berthollet's Canary example was twenty-five inches long; Storer quotes the dimensions of the New England ones at two feet; and Mr. Beattie's Forfar one measures twenty-two inches and three-quarters. These dimensions approach those of the Tunnies, and sailors very commonly confound the Striped Thynni and the Pelamids with each other under the general term of Bonitos; they also give them the name of Skip-jacks, expressive of the habit which many of the large Scomberoids have of skimming the surface of the sea, and springing occasionally into the air.

Pallas describes the Black Sea Pelamids as being vari-

c 2

20 SCOMBRIDÆ.

ously clouded, on the upper parts, with brown and blue bands, while the under parts are silvery white and highly polished, and he adds that a blue stripe runs along under the lateral line. The branchiostegous membrane and the first dorsal are black, the pectoral fins azure-coloured—the purity of the colours and elegant form of the fish rendering it a very beautiful object.

The British Scomberoid to which the Pelamid has the nearest resemblance in external form is the Belted Bonito, which has been detected in our seas by Mr. Couch alone: but that Thynnus has shorter teeth, and only thirteen spinous rays, in the first dorsal. In the Forfarshire specimen the following is the formula of the rays—

Br. 7: D. 21—1+13—viii.: A. 4+12—vi.: P. 24: V. 1+5: C. 21—20.

The spinous rays of the first dorsal are slender, and the third is the tallest, while the first is not above a sixth or a seventh part shorter. The figure shows the form of the fin, and how it falls off posteriorly. There is, perhaps, a short incumbent ray on the base of the second dorsal spine, but its existence cannot be proved without dissection, and it may be that the spine is merely thickened at the base. The numbers of the detached finlets behind the dorsal and anal vary with the age of the fish in the Scomberoids, the membrane being more continuous in the young, and including more of them. Four slender, graduated, jointless rays commence the anal. The pectoral is triangular, and when in repose, fits into a depression of the corselet. Its tip, when laid back, just passes the eighth ray of the first dorsal: and the ventrals, which also recline in a cutaneous depression, have their origin opposite to the base of the first pectoral ray. The corselet composed of scales, larger and

THE PELAMID. 21

somewhat more conspicuous than the others, covers a triangular area on each side, which extends from the supra-scapula to a little beyond the point of the pectoral, where it ends rather obtusely. Its inferior edge is straight, and running along and near the under margin of the pectoral, joins the coracoid above the curve of the gill-cover. On the back the scales are very small, but sufficiently visible to the naked eye by reflected light, particularly a row or two under the spinous dorsal. They become gradually imperceptible on the sides, and are lost on the belly in the smooth nacry integument.

In the supra-scapular region, the lateral line bounds the corselet, receding from it over the proximal third of the pectoral, in a small curve convex upwards, then, before it passes the posterior third of the pectoral, resuming a straight course parallel to the back and nearer to its profile than to that of the belly. It makes, however, some slight undulations before reaching the region of the vent. Opposite the penultimate dorsal and anal free finlets, the lateral line is replaced by a callous cutaneous crest, which terminates at the base of the caudal. There are no oblique crests on the bases of the fin just named, such as the Common Mackerel possesses.

Both jaws are armed by conico-subulate teeth, rather widely set, with smaller ones springing up in some of the intervals. Most of these teeth are moderately curved, and the tallest ones arm the sides of the mandible; a pair, equally tall, however, stands on each side of the point of that bone, and rather more interiorly than the general row. On the premaxillaries the teeth are smaller and closer. The palatine ones are strongly curved and rather crowded: there are none on the vomer.

Ten dark bars traverse the back and upper half of

SCOMBRIDÆ.

the sides, descending below the lateral line. They run obliquely, the longest one extending from between the first and second free dorsal finlets to the apex of the corselet; the others lie parallel to it and at equal distances, and consequently, owing to the curve of the back, decrease in length the further they are situated from the one above mentioned. In the dried specimen the cheek is impressed by brownish grooves or wrinkles, intercepting elliptical areas, and similar depressions exist on the integument covering the coracoids. On the head generally, and especially on the jaws and gill-covers, the skin is very smooth, even, and nacry, without scales. The branchiostegous membrane and the isthmus of the gills are bluish-black. The first dorsal also appears to have been blackish. Including the caudal, the specimen measures twenty-one and three-quarter inches in length.

In the Zoologist for 1859 (p. 6731) mention is made of the capture, in a herring-net set off the coast of Banff, of an example of the Plain Bonito (*Auxis vulgaris* of the second edition)—a fish which has hitherto been but seldom recognised on our coasts.

In the warmer districts of the Atlantic, Bonitos, Pelamids, and other large Scomberoids, are fished for with tackle rigged like a Mackerel line, but considerably stronger. The bait is a piece of bright tin, shaped like a Flying-fish, or a slice of the skin of pork, or of the tail of a Mackerel. The hook is weighted so as to sink a little beneath the surface of the water, and produces most sport when it is dragged at the rate of five miles an hour, or thereabouts.

ACANTHOPTERI. SCOMBRIDÆ.

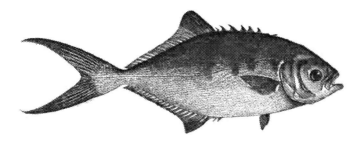

THE DERBIO.

Lichia glaucus, Cuv. et Valenc. viii. p. 558, pl. 234.
Premier glaucus, Rondelet, p. 252.
Lampuge des Marseillais, Belon, p. 155.
Scomber glaucus, Linnæus.
Gasterosteus glaucus, Forster, Des. An. p. 5.
Centronotus vel *Lichia glaycos,* Risso, 2me Edit.
Centronotus binotatus, Rafinesque.
Albacore, Couch, Linn. Tr. xiv. p. 82. Jenyns, Man. p. 366.

Lichia. *Generic Characters.*—Form oval, compressed, covered with leathery scales, without keel or lateral ridges on the tail; head small; teeth minute. Dorsal spines low, isolated, each with an axillary membrane, and, in front of all, a recumbent spine; two preanal spines; second dorsal and anal long, similar to one another; no spurious fins. Seven branchiostegals. A large air-bladder, expanded posteriorly. Five conspicuous cranial ridges, the median one being the longest and highest.

Four species of this genus are described in the *Histoire des Poissons,* three of them inhabitants of the Mediterranean, but together with the fourth, ranging also along the western coast of Africa, some of them as far as the Cape of Good Hope, where the Dutch colonists call them *lyre-vish.* The species which we have to describe is the one which Rondelet says is known at Montpellier, by the name of *Derbio,* but which is called *La liche* and *La cabrolle* by the Provençals, and *La lechia* by

24   SCOMBRIDÆ.

the Sards and Romans. At Nice its name is *lecco*, and, according to Rafinesque, its Sicilian appellations are *cionana*, *ciodena* and *ciodera*. Cuvier received specimens from various Atlantic localities, Algesiras, Madeira, Teneriffe, Goree, Ascension, Saint Helena, the Cape of Good Hope, and from Brazil, not to be distinguished from the Mediterranean ones. It may possibly be, as Forster intimates, the *Sea-blueling* or *Silver-fish* of the West Indies, but we have seen no example from that quarter. It occurs in the Rev. R. T. Lowe's list of Madeira fish, under the local names of *Ranhosa*, *Toonbeta*, and *Pelumbeta*, and is said to be extremely common at that island. It belongs to the same tribe of Scomberoids, with free dorsal spines, as *Naucrates*, that is, to the *Centronoti* of Lacépède.

Notwithstanding its extensive southern range, it seems to wander rarely into the more northern parts of the Atlantic. It is not mentioned by French ichthyologists as having been captured on the western coasts of their country; and Mr. Couch, to whose industry and acute discrimination British Ichthyology owes so much, is the only person who has procured an English specimen. That solitary example is carefully preserved in the Museum of the Natural History Society of Penzance, and we have not had an opportunity of seeing it, but through the kindness of Dr. Gray, of the British Museum, we have been enabled to compare two excellent photographs of the specimen with the figures given in the *Histoire des Poissons*, and in Webb and Bertholet's *Histoire Naturelle des Isles Canaries*. (Poiss. pl. 13.) With the latter the photograph agrees so closely as to leave no doubt of the specific identity of the fish they represent, and the former differs merely in the lateral line, being a little more undulated anteriorly. The lateral spots are not exhibited in the photograph, its prototype being, probably, too young

THE DERBIO. 25

for the development of these markings. Cuvier regards the *Lichia tetracantha* discovered by Mr. Bowdich near the Gambia as merely a variety of this species, but from a drawing of *tetracantha* made at Sierra Leone by Dr. Mitchill, Surgeon in the Royal Navy, it appears to be a considerably more oblong species, and instead of about four spots on the fore part of the sides, there is a series of ten smaller ones, extending nearly to the base of the caudal. Its colour is bright ultramarine blue, and silvery white below, the lateral spots being darker blue, and the tips of the fins blackish-blue, as in *glaucus*. The true *glaucus* was also obtained by Dr. Mitchill, off the Niger in the Bight of Benin, and his drawing represents it as of a darker blue than *tetracantha*, and of a considerably deeper oval form. The following description of the Derbio is drawn up from the photographs, with additions furnished by Mr. Couch.

This gentleman states the length of the specimen to have been thirteen inches and a half, and its height three inches and seven-eighths. The comparative length, omitting the acute caudal lobes, is thrice the height; and the head forms a sixth part of the total length, including the whole caudal fin. The scales are small, and not strong. The cheeks nacry and scaleless. The lateral line descends obliquely without an abrupt curve from the suprascapular, till it comes nearly over the first free anal spine, and a little above mid-height, and from thence runs straight to the central rays of the caudal fin without any keeling or armature perceptible in the photograph.

The fin formula is—

D. VI.—1 + 22: A. II.—1 + 23 or 24.

The ventrals and pectorals are both small. There is a couchant spine pointing forwards before the first dorsal, which is composed of six detached spines, all nearly of

26 SCOMBRIDÆ.

equal height, and each with a triangular membrane in its axilla. The soft dorsal and anal are alike, each being higher in front, but not decidedly falcate, and each having a short spine incumbent on the base of the first articulated ray. Two detached spines stand in front of the anal similar to those of the first dorsal, and midway between them and the ventrals is the vent.

The caudal is deeply swallow-tailed.

There are several vertical oval spots or bars in a row just above the lateral line, and touching it. These are said in the *Histoire des Poissons* to be peculiar to the adult fish. Mr. Couch says, that the dorsal aspect and the lateral bars were of rather a dark blue; the ventral aspect from the mandible to the caudal, and including the eye, was pale yellow, and the dark blotches on the anterior tips of the soft dorsal and anal were well marked. Cuvier describes the air-bladder as forked posteriorly, its long points entering among the muscles of the tail on each side of the anal interspinal bones : and he considers the course of the lateral line without a decided elbow as a mark by which the Derbio may be readily distinguished from the *Lichia amia*, which is the second *glaucus* of Ronde-let, the *amia* of Salviani, and the *cerviola* of the Sicilians. In this second species the lateral line has a strong curva-ture in form of the letter ∽. Willughby introduced much confusion into the history of these two species, having mistaken the Derbio or the first *glaucus* of Ron-delet for the second one; and Ray, Artedi, and Linnæus have all, while correct on some points, fallen into error on others in their accounts of the several species of Lichia.

ACANTHOPTERI. *TÆNIÆDÆ.*

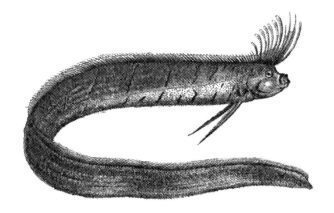

BANKS'S OAR-FISH.

Regalecus Banksii, GRAY, Pr. Zool. Soc. for 1849, p. 80.
Gymnetrus Banksii, CUV. et VALENC. Poiss. x. p. 365.

REGALECUS. *Generic Characters.*—Greatly compressed and elongated sword-shaped fishes. Teeth minute or none. Dorsal fin rising on the occiput like a plume. Caudal said to be continuous with the dorsal, and to embrace the point of the tail, but seldom seen entire, and of doubtful form in most species. Ventrals uni-radiate and very long, edged with membrane which expands at the end. Branchiostegals seven. A very long slender tapering stomach, of which three-fourths is cæcal; pancreatic cæca simple and very numerous. Scales microscopical in the nacry epidermis, also scattered osteoid tubercles in the skin. No air-bladder.

IN the Banksian library at the end of a quarto copy of Pennant's British Zoology, published in 1776, is the following manuscript note:—" On Saturday, the 23rd day of February 1788, was caught near Newlyn Quay, on the sand at ebb-tide, a fish which measured in length eight feet four inches, in breadth ten inches, and thickness two inches and a half; its weight was forty pounds." Another marginal note states further that "a gentleman

TÆNIÆDÆ.

who saw this fish informed Capt. Chemming (Chelwyn ? or Chirgwin ?) that the tail was not perfect." A figure which accompanied these notices has been reproduced in part, and of reduced size, by Dr. Gray, in a paper published in the Proceedings of the Zoological Society, for May 29, 1849. In this the front ray of the dorsal fin standing on the forehead between the eyes is very long and tapering, and curves forward before the face : the following ten rays diminish successively in length, and are not represented as being connected by membrane : the rest of the dorsal is comparatively low, and has only the tips of the rays rising above the continuous membrane. The ventrals have each one long ray dilated into a broadly-oval pallette, apparently of membrane, folded or radiated.

Pasted into the same copy of Pennant there is also a paragraph cut from the York Chronicle, stating that on the 18th of March 1796 four women picked up a curious and uncommon fish, which came ashore in Filey Bay. They sold it to a man who carried it to York. Sir Joseph Banks's correspondent sent him a tracing of a drawing of the fish by Dr. Burgh, together with observations which are here abridged from Dr. Gray's paper :— " Thirteen feet long, one foot deep, three inches thick, head seven inches long, eye one inch three-eighths in diameter. The dorsal fin runs from the head to the other end, at which there is no tail; it has 290 and 13 rays, and is red like that of a roach or perch ; the pectoral has twelve ; the ventral one; no anal. Branchiostegous rays six. No teeth, a soft tongue. Anus, four feet nine inches from the head. The face, and inside of the mouth, black ; the irides silvery white. Though there was no caudal fin when I saw it, it is not clear that he never had one, for there was an appearance of mutilation in its place.—W. B."

Notices of the capture on our coasts of similar fish,

BANKS'S OAR-FISH. 29

but mostly too imperfect for the identification of species, occur in various periodicals. The Annual Register records the taking of one of these at Whitby on the 22nd of January 1759; and Mr. Stanton of Newcastle informed Messrs. Hancock and Embleton, that about the end of the 18th century he recollected the exhibition of a similar fish in Newcastle. It was ten feet long, and two inches thick. A sketch was made of it by Bewick the celebrated wood-engraver, which has been unfortunately mislaid. The same gentlemen were told by John Blackett Anderson, of Walker, near Newcastle, that he recollects the capture of two fishes about the year 1800, in a shallow pool at the outer Fern Islands. The larger was eighteen feet long, about a foot deep, and of a silvery colour. In 1796 one was got at Cullercoats, near Newcastle, as mentioned in a pamphlet published in 1849 by John Such, of that town. On the 19th of March 1844, one was stranded, after a severe north-east gale, at the village of Crovie, in the estuary of the Doveran, near Macduff in Banffshire, and was afterwards exhibited in the Town-hall of Elgin. From the correspondence of Mr. John Martin of the "Elgin Institution," with the late Dr. Johnston of Berwick, and the sketches he sent, Mr. Yarrell entertained no doubt of its specific identity with the *Regalecus* to be fully described below, and whose portrait is placed at the commencement of this article. Mr. Martin states the measurements of the Crovie specimen to be, total length twelve feet; depth one foot; thickness two inches and three-quarters; height of the dorsal fin two inches and a half, length of the ventral rays three feet; length of the pectorals two inches and a half. The head measured nine inches from the symphysis of the mandible to the end of the gill-cover; and from thence to the vent the distance was forty-six inches. There was no caudal fin. The

30 TÆNIÆDÆ.

shaft of each ventral was about the thickness of a goose-quill, was fringed on each side by membrane, and broken short off at the extremity; the ends having been thrown away at the sea-side, their original length could not be ascertained. The dorsal fin contained two hundred and seventy-nine rays, of which fifteen standing on the head were very tall, but were connected at the base by membrane. The pectorals were supported by twelve rays. The lateral line was straight, and about one-third of the height above the ventral profile, except where it rose gradually over the pectorals. The body is described, and the drawings represent it, as having a slightly-tapering profile from the operculum to the end, which is rather abrupt, with a spur at its lower corner, and without any indication of a caudal fin. If one existed, Mr. Martin thinks that it must have been very slender. The whole body was clothed by a delicate white skin with a silvery lustre, beneath which there lay alternate smooth and tuberculated bands running the whole length of the body, palpable to the finger through the outer skin, and becoming more perceptible on its removal. Behind the pectoral fin, a few dark bars, which crossed the body obliquely, were very conspicuous when the fish was fresh, and the dorsal had at first an orange tint.

Messrs. Hancock and Embleton's paper mentions that one of the Preventive Service men, in the year 1845, observed a fish of this kind in a pool near Alnmouth. On his approach it bent its body into a circle, and he, ignorantly thinking that it was going to spring upon him, boldly attacked it with his cutlass and cut off its head. It was sixteen feet long, eleven inches deep, and six thick. In the struggles of the dying fish, the sands around were covered with its delicate nacry scales.

BANKS'S OAR-FISH.

On the 26th of March 1849, a fine fish of this genus was captured by the crew of a fishing coble belonging to Cullercoats, consisting of Bartholomew Taylor and his two sons. It was much injured by the captors in their endeavours to secure it, and by subsequent handling during its exhibition at Tynemouth, North and South Shields, and Newcastle. Fortunately it was seen at the last-named town by Albany Hancock, Esq., and Dr. Dennis Embleton, who made drawings of it, and drew up a detailed account of its external appearance and internal structure, which was read at a meeting of the Tyneside Naturalists' Club, and published in the Annals and Magazine of Natural History for July 1849. From that paper the following abridged extracts are taken by permission.

The fish, though much injured and greatly faded, was fresh and had a uniform silvery-grey colour, except a few irregular streaks and dark spots towards the fore-part of the body, and there were remains of a bright iridescence about the pectoral fin and head, a blue tint predominating. The body is excessively compressed, like a double-edged sword-blade, its greatest thickness being below the middle, and the dorsal edge is sharper than the ventral one. The total length when the mouth is retracted is twelve feet three inches, and the depth immediately behind the gills eight inches and a half: two feet farther back the greatest depth of eleven inches and a quarter is attained, and at the end of the dorsal fin it has diminished to three. The skin is covered with a silvery matter in which the scales are invisible to the naked eye, but which is easily detached and adheres to anything it comes in contact with. Submitted to the microscope, this nacre was found to consist of scales like those on the wing of a moth. Round the hind border of the operculum there is a broad dusky patch; a crescentic dark mark exists

32 TÆNIÆDÆ.

above the eye, and there are eight or nine narrow oblique streaks on the side, which diminish to mere spots beyond the vent. The lateral line descends gradually from the suprascapula to within two inches of the ventral profile at the vent, and continues descending as it proceeds to the distal end of the fish. Four flattened ridges, each more than an inch in breadth, reach from the head to the tail above the lateral line, the longest and uppermost commencing near the eye. The skin is studded with numerous bony tubercles not regularly arranged, and in the neighbourhood of the head they are replaced by depressed indurations. On the ventral edge the tubercles are numerous and have hooked tips pointing towards the tail.

The head is small, measuring only nine inches to the gill-opening; the orifice of the mouth is circular and capable of being protruded two or three inches by the depression of the mandible. The tongue is small, smooth, and prominent; there are no teeth, and the interior of the mouth is black. Gill-plates proportionally large, preoperculum crescentic, with the lower horn prolonged forwards to the articulation of the mandible. Operculum curved elliptically posteriorly, ending obtusely. Branchiostegals seven. Branchial arches four, with tubercular bristly rakers. Pharyngeal bones above and below furnished with setaceous teeth.

The dorsal fin extends from between the front of the orbits to within three inches of the distal extremity of the fish. The twelve anterior rays were stated by the captors to have been about fourteen inches long, and furnished with a membrane on their posterior edges, which grew wider upwards, somewhat like a peacock's feather. The ends were broken off, but a continuous membrane connected their bases, and their shafts appeared ragged

BANKS'S OAR-FISH.

with the remains of the torn membrane. In addition to these there were 268 other rays whose acute points overtopped the connecting membrane, or 280 dorsal rays in all. About the middle of the fish, where the dorsal rays are highest, excepting those on the head, they measure upwards of three inches and a half, and at the termination of the fin their height has decreased to one inch. Behind the termination of the dorsal fin the edge of the back slopes rapidly downwards to within an inch of the line of the belly, and then forms a rounded point which is the distal extremity of the fish. Both the upper and under edges of this extremity are very thin, and the fishermen insisted that when they took the fish this part was entire, and that there was no tail-fin whatever. The edges may be pressed together, and seem to fit. The pectorals are attached low, and contain eleven rays. The ventral fins were represented by a pair of very strong straight spines broken short to the length of four inches, but were said to have been originally twice that length, having even then broken ends; a membranous edge was visible at their bases. The vertebræ, judging from elevations obscurely seen through the muscles, were reckoned at 110. Fin-ray formula—

D. 280 : V. 1 : P. 11. Vertebræ 110?—*Hancock and Embleton, l.c.*

Messrs. Hancock and Embleton's excellent paper may be consulted for the internal anatomical structure, and several particulars of external form, which have been omitted here from want of space.*

In 1850, another example of this fish, alive but mutilated, was cast ashore on the Yorkshire coast, near Redcar. It measured nearly twelve feet, and weighed sixty-six pounds, as reported in the *Zoologist* (2709) by T. S.

* For a larger cut of the head copied from this paper, see foot of page 35.

VOL. I. (*2nd Supp.*) D

34   TÆNIÆDÆ.

Rudd, Esq. In the same communication, mention is made of one found on that coast several years previously by a pilot named Slater Potts: if its length was correctly stated at twenty-four feet, it is the largest example of this species that has been recorded. Another was stranded on the 17th of September 1852, near Millar's Stone, in the Bay of Cromarty. This specimen was secured for the museum of Mr. Dunbar at Inverness, and on the dispersion of that collection some years ago, came into the hands of a bird-stuffer of the same place, who kept it hanging in his shop until he tired of looking at it, and no purchaser offering, it was at length consigned by him to the dust-cart.

A northern member of this genus was described by Ascanius under the name of *Ophidium Glesne* in the Copenhagen Memoirs for 1776, the generic name being afterwards changed to *Regalecus*, by which he intended to signify King of the Herrings. Glesne is the name of a village near Bergen, where the fish was taken. This species, which received other names from ichthyologists who came after Ascanius, has been supposed to be the same with the British fish; and the case may be so, but hitherto the Norwegian fish has been described by Ascanius and Brünnich alone, and the one reckons only 126 rays in the dorsal fin, and the other 197, while the figures given by these authors show a greater number. This reckoning, however, is so different from the numbers of the rays in the British fish, that they cannot be considered as the same species until the mistake, if there be one, has been rectified by an accurate examination and comparison of specimens. *Gymnetrus Grillii* of Lindroth, described in 1798, had the large number of 406 dorsal rays, with a total length of eighteen feet, and ventrals measuring five. It is therefore safer for the present to keep Messrs. Hancock and Embleton's fish distinct under the name of *Banksii,* proposed by M. Valenciennes in the *Histoire des Poissons.* The right of priority over the term *Gymnetrus* belongs to *Regalecus,* and this is therefore used here, though M. Valenciennes rejects it for its barbarity.

BANKS'S OAR-FISH (Hancock and Embleton).

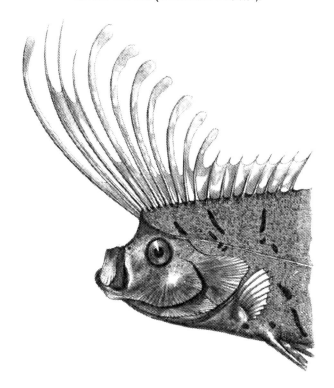

JAWS OF COUCH'S SEA-BREAM. See page 5.

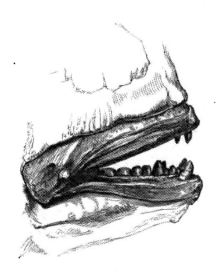

END OF SECOND SUPPLEMENT
TO FIRST VOLUME.

SECOND SUPPLEMENT

TO THE SECOND VOLUME OF

THE HISTORY OF BRITISH FISHES.

ANACANTHINI.
ANISOMERI.
PLEURONECTIDÆ.

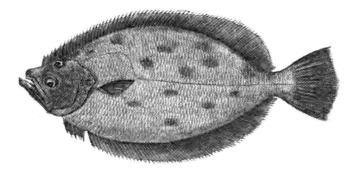

THE SAIL-FLUKE.

Zeugopterus? velivolans. EDITOR of the Third Ed. of Br. Fishes.

DR. BAIKIE, writing from the banks of the Niger, referred to Dr. Alex. Duguid of Kirkwall for information respecting the very curious habits of this fish, and that gentleman, on being applied to, most kindly sent a sketch made by a friend of his, said to be very correct, from which the above wood-cut has been engraved. He also furnished the following particulars of the history of the fish. This Fluke, he says, is highly prized as an article of food, its flesh being firm and white. It does not take a bait, and he only once saw it caught in a net, but it comes ashore, spontaneously, with its tail erected above the water, like a boat under sail, whence its name. This it does generally in calm weather, and on sandy shores, and the country people residing near such places train

PLEURONECTIDÆ.

their dogs to catch it. The following letter was written by Mr. Robert Scarth, of North Ronaldshay, the northernmost island of the Orkney group, where the Sail-fluke is very common:—" It is never caught by hook or by net, and I have in vain set ground lines for it in the South Bay, baited with Lug-worms, Limpets and Sellocks, neither have Flounder or Skate nets, drawn there, inclosed a Sail-fluke. It seldom comes to the shore earlier than October or later than April, though it is often driven by storms on the beach, entangled among sea-weed. The great supply is, however, obtained in the following manner:—In the winter and early spring a pair of Black-headed Gulls take possession of the Bay, drive away all interlopers, and may be seen at daybreak every morning beating from side to side, on the wing, and never both in one place, except in the act of crossing as they pass. The Sail-fluke skims the ridge of the wave towards the shore with its tail raised over its back, and when the wave recedes is left on the sand, into which it burrows so suddenly and completely, that though I have watched its approach, only once have I succeeded in finding its burrow. The Gull, however, has a surer eye, and casting like a hawk, pounces on the Fluke, from which by one stroke of his bill it extracts the liver. If not disturbed, the Gull no sooner gorges this luscious morsel, than it commences dragging the fish to some outlying rock, where he and his consort may discuss it at leisure. By robbing the Black-backs I have had the house supplied daily with this excellent fish, in weather during which no fishing-boat could put to sea. Close to the beach of South Bay a stone wall has been raised to shelter the crops from the sea-spray. Behind this we posted a smart lad, who kept his eye on the soaring Gulls. The moment one of the birds made its well-known swoop, the boy rushed

THE SAIL-FLUKE. 3

to the sea-strand, shouting with all his might. He was usually in time to scare the Gull away and secure the Fluke, but in almost every case with the liver torn out. If the Gull by chance succeeded in carrying his prey off to the rock, he and his partner set up a triumphant cackling, as if deriding the disappointed lad. Seals often pursue these Flukes into the bay, and frequently leave serviceable morsels unconsumed. The Sail-fluke exhibits its gambols most frequently before a storm, or when a thaw succeeds a frost. It is the most delicious fish of our seas, but loses its flavour by a day's keeping."—19 Feb. 1849.

Length of a specimen, twenty-one inches. Height, excluding the fins, seven inches and a half, or including them, ten inches. Weight three pounds.

D. 87 : A. 69 : P. 11 : V. 5 : C. 19½.

The dorsal commences before the upper eye, which is three-quarters of an inch before the lower one. The rough lateral line is much arched over the pectoral fin. Scales large and striated from the centre, roughish on the pale belly, and very small on the fronts of the fin-rays. There is one row of minute sharp teeth on each jaw, and also some teeth on the vomer. Tongue round and conical. Operculum and interoperculum thin and very diaphanous, the bony plates, and the cheeks being as thin as silk paper, so that the smallest type may be read through them. The left or coloured side of the fish is like that of the Common Dab, yellowish-brown, with scattered dark blotches.—Another specimen weighed four pounds, and had ninety-one dorsal rays, with seventy-five anal ones.—(*Dr. Duguid.*)

The oval of the body is wider vertically than that of the *Smähvarf* (Pl. 50) of the *Scandinaviens Fiskar*, but narrower than the ovals of either of our English Top-knots. In the facial profile and forms of the vertical fins there is

E 2

much similarity between the Smähvarf and the Sail-fluke, but none of the four specimens of the former, noticed by Sundevall, have so many dorsal and anal rays as the Orkney Fluke. In the latter, also, the upper eye is more distinctly behind the lower one, and the mandible protrudes farther. Sundevall makes no mention of transparent cheeks; for the present, therefore, they are described as distinct, such a proceeding being less injurious to science than the junction of two species divers in structure and habits under one name. In the absence of a specimen, the Sail-fluke is placed in the genus *Zeugopterus* interrogatively. A single row of jaw-teeth only is mentioned by Dr. Duguid, but he probably means laterally, where the Smähvarf has only one row, though there is a crowded patch at the symphyses of its jaws.

SUGAR-LOAF, SUTHERLANDSHIRF.

ACANTHOPTERI. GOBIESOCIDÆ.

THE CONNEMARA SUCKER.

Lepidogaster cephalus, THOMPS. Nat. Hist. of Irel. iii. p. 214.

THE authority for this species is a specimen, which was taken in Roundstone Bay, Connemara, on the western coast of Ireland, and is preserved in the collection of the late Dr. Ball of Dublin. It has not been observed on the English coasts, nor has any drawing been made of it to which we have access. Mr. Thompson published an account of it in the Annals of Natural History (iii. 34), which has been reprinted in the posthumous edition of his work above quoted. The following passages are extracted from his paper.

" This fish equals *Lepidogaster Cornubiensis* in size, but differs from it in the dorsal and anal fins occupying a considerable portion of its length, and in having a greater breadth of head with a narrower snout: the body like-wise is more depressed, and narrows more suddenly be-hind the ventral disk into the tapering tail. Its specific characters are—a very minute cirrus before each eye; dorsal and anal fins unconnected with the caudal; ven-tral disk small.

Br. 5 : D. 15 : A. 10 : P. 25 and 4 : C. 15 conspicuous, 20 in all.

" Head very broad posteriorly, forming more than one-third of the entire length; in front of each orbit, and on a line with its upper border, there is a cirrus so minute as to be scarcely visible without the aid of a lens; eyes large, two of their diameters apart: teeth pointed and numerous on the jaws, the outer premaxillary ones being the largest; gill-opening small; ventral disk smaller, and different from that of *L. Cornubiensis.* Dorsal fin originating behind the middle of the fish, and continued to near the caudal, with which it does not unite; anal fin commencing farther back, but reaching as far; the last rays of the two fins, when laid down, touching the base of the caudal: rays of all the fins jointed, but not branched: vent situated midway between the posterior edge of the ventral disk and the end of the caudal fin: a short anal tubercle."—*Thompson, l. c.*

The *Lepidogaster Webbianus* of Valenciennes, which inhabits the seas of the Canary Islands, has two cutaneous filaments at the nostrils on each side, and so has also the *L. zebrinus* of Lowe, which inhabits the Madeira coasts, and is perhaps the same species with *Webbianus.* The *Lepidogaster chupasangue* of the same seas, which Mr. Lowe thinks may be *L. Decandollii* of Risso, has no nasal cirrus, and the vertical fins are not connected to each other.

VIEW OF LANCRIGG.

GANOIDEI. *ACIPENSERIDÆ.*

THE COMMON BRITISH STURGEON.

Acipenser Thompsoni, Ball, Thompson's Nat. Hist. of Ireland, iii. 245.
,, *sturio, Common Sturgeon,* Penn. Brit. Zool. iii. 164, pl. 22.
,, ,, ,, ,, Donov. Brit. Fish. pl. 55.
,, ,, ,, ,, Jenyns, Man. 493.
,, ,, *Sturgeon,* Flem. Brit. Anim. 173.

Acipenseridæ. *Family Characters.*—Form elongated, pentagonal; the angles of the body formed by the crests of five longitudinal rows of bony shields; mouth on the ventral aspect, protractile, toothless; no branchiostegals; internal skeleton cartilaginous, except the basal cephalic plate of bone, which extends backwards under the first five dorsal vertebræ; vertical fins supported anteriorly by short bony rays; a long spiral intestinal valve; pancreas glandular.

Acipenser. *Generic Characters.*—Snout tapering, beak-shaped, with four barbels depending from its ventral surface before the mouth; an accessory gill, and, at the upper border of the gill-cover, a spout-hole; trunk of the tail not flattened.—*Heckel.*

The Sturgeons are Ganoid fishes of a lengthened shape, having a cartilaginous skeleton, and the protractile mouth situated under the eyes on the ventral surface considerably behind the tip of the snout. The jaws are much more protractile than those of a Shark, and consist of the premaxillaries going round the upper or anterior border of the mouth, with small maxillaries articulated to them laterally and connected also to the palatines. The mandible is formed principally of a pair of bony limbs, united to each other at the symphysis, ending laterally in a joint furnished with a trochlear cartilage, and moving on the wing-like process of each palatine. A thick fleshy lip, sometimes lobed, covers the premaxillaries; but the mandibular lip is deficient in some groups of species, except at the corners of the mouth; and in other groups the posterior lip crosses the orifice, either in form of a continuous soft roll, or with a mesial depression, or even a mesial interspace The fulness of the lips, in conjunction with the forms of the dorsal crests and a few other characters, have been made to serve for grouping the species. The gills, as in the osseous fishes, consist of five movable arches, and are comb-like, with free tips: a pectinated accessory gill also adheres to the inner surface of the gill-cover, and there is a small spout-hole close behind and above it.

Of the five rows of bony shields on the body, one protects the ridge of the back from the occiput to the dorsal fin; a lateral row extends on each flank from the shoulder to the caudal fin; and a row on each side of the belly ends at the ventrals. Each dorsal shield is more or less distinctly keeled by an acute longitudinal crest, whose apex, in some groups of species, overhangs the posterior edge of the shield, but in other groups is central, the plate sloping off from it both before and behind. The skin intervening between the rows of shields varies also in character, being naked and smooth, or studded with bony grains, either of a granular form, or star-shaped, or with acute points or even hooks. In *Ac. Güldenstädii* of Brandt, which is the *Ac. sturio* of Pallas, the skin of the breast between the coracoid shields is set with elevated star-like or roundish and denticulated ossicles; while in *Ac. nasus* of Heckel the same region is closely covered with flat ganoid scales, like those of *Lepidosteus*. In *Ac. schypa* of Güldenstädt the same part shows stellate ossicles,

THE COMMON BRITISH STURGEON.

9

many of which emit prickles. The *Schypa* is var. β and γ of the *Sturio* of Pallas, who obtained it in the Wolga and Obi.

Age changes the form and size of the body-shields of the Sturgeons, their crests becoming lower and blunter, and their disks smaller, so that in aged fish the sharply-pentagonal form of the body is lost, and the ventral shields often wholly disappear.

The fins, seven in number, are sustained by crowded jointed, and generally flexible rays, finely serrated on the edges; the short graduated rays in front of the dorsal and anal are more or less bony. The anal is situated under the posterior part of the dorsal, which is itself placed far back. A stout, tall, bony first ray supports the pectoral fin.

The skull is cartilaginous throughout, but is supported beneath by an osseous occipito-sphenoidal plate, which extends posteriorly under five cervical vertebræ, and is prolonged anteriorly into a slender vomerine and ethmoidal process; protection is afforded to the skull above by a vaulted crust of ganoid scales or shields, which have received names from Kittary,[*] Fitzinger and Heckel [†] and others, accordant with the regions that they cover. [‡] In the views of the upper surface of the head introduced in the subsequent pages, the posterior mesial shield is the first of the dorsal series; anterior to it is the single occipital shield also occupying a mesial place; and whose anterior process enters some way between the coronal or parietal shields which form a pair and come in contact

---

[*] Dr. Modeste Kittary: Bull. de la Soc. Imp. des Natur. de Moscov. 1850.

[†] Annalen der Wien. Erster Band.

[‡] Professor Owen observes that the attempt to ascertain the homologies of these cranial shields with the true epicranial bones of osseous fishes is difficult and unsatisfactory.

10 ACIPENSERIDÆ.

with each other for a part of their length; before the coronals and between the eyes lie the frontal shields forming another pair; in the Frith of Forth Narrow-nosed Sturgeon the frontals are wholly separated by one or more interfrontal plates; the postfrontal and prefrontal shields are exterior to the main frontals in the positions that their names indicate; laterally with respect to the coronals lie the temporal shields, often coalescent with a squamosal piece; and behind them occupying the posterior lateral angles of the head, and protecting on each side a styloid process of the cartilaginous skull (which Owen terms a representation of the par-occipital, but which Kittary calls the mastoid), lies a shield that articulates with the first dorsal, the occipital, and squamosal, and the suprascapular: the last-named shield being the first of the humeral chain that descends behind the gill-opening, heads the lateral series of body-shields, all of which partake of its scalene form; the chevron-shaped humeral shield gives support to the bony ray of the pectoral; and the coracoid, the largest piece of the humeral chain, has wholly a ventral aspect, its crest being on a line with the crests of the ventral body-shields; the suprascapular, opercular, and such cranial shields as have a lateral aspect, are represented in the profiles of the head.

The arterial bulb of the Sturgeons is furnished with two rows of valves at its commencement, and with one row at its termination. The swim-bladder is very large, and communicates with the gullet by a wide hole. In the glandular conglomeration of their pancreatic cæca the Sturgeons resemble the Sharks.

Heckel and Kner* divide the genus into six groups, three of which, viz. the *Lionisci*, *Acipenserini*, and *Helopes*, have the dorsal shields highest at their posterior edges, and the

* Süssw. Fische der Östreich. Mon. 1858.

THE COMMON BRITISH STURGEON. 11

two first-named have, moreover, fringed barbels, characters which have been attributed to no British Sturgeon. In the other three groups, *Antacei, Sturiones,* and *Husones,* the ridges of the dorsal shields are pointed in the middle, and slope down anteriorly and posteriorly. These groups are further characterized as follows :—4. *Antacei,* having simple and not fringed barbels, a rudimentary mandibular lip, the skin between the rows of body-shields studded with stellate ossicles, and the snout short and broad. 5. *Sturiones,* having a swollen posterior lip, contracted in the middle, simple barbels, and the skin between the rows of body-shields granulated by blunt ossicles. 6. *Husones,* having the mandibular lip divided in the middle ; flat, tape-like barbels, and the skin roughened by pointed ossicles. The species are distinguished from each other by the relative positions of the osseous centres of their principal cranial shields. With respect to the value for this purpose of the form of the shields, Dr. Ball says :— " I have collected many specimens, and I do not think that the broadness or sharpness of the nose is a specific distinction, as no two of my specimens can be said to agree in the shape of that member, nor in the arrangement of the scales on it and on the head. A classification of the variations of my numerous examples will reduce the British *Sturio, Thompsoni* and *latirostris* to a single species." Mr. Thompson also observes that " the precise form of the bony plates on the head is of no value as a specific character, neither is the breadth of the snout." These opinions of the Irish naturalists are shared by several English ichthyologists, and the subject requires to be worked out by an investigator who has access to a sufficient number of examples from various British localities, and an opportunity of comparing them with specimens collected from the Continental rivers.

ACIPENSERIDÆ.

Bloch's figure is worthless from the want of correct details.

Sturgeons named, evidently from their size, *Stör, Storje, Stoer,* and *Storjer,* by the Scandinavians, inhabit the Baltic, the German Ocean, the English and Irish Channels, and the Mediterranean, Black Sea, Caspian, and Baikal. They abound also in the waters of North America which fall into the Atlantic and Pacific, but they do not appear to frequent rivers which flow into the icy seas. They feed at the bottom, in deep water, beyond the ordinary reach of sea-nets, and are therefore very rarely taken, except in friths, estuaries, or rivers, which they enter for the purpose of spawning. They are more frequently captured in the Scottish waters than on the southern coasts of England, and have been taken, according to Thompson, in the Irish counties of Cork, Derry, Kilkenny, Wexford, Dublin, Down, and Antrim. Examples are by no means uncommon in the fishmongers' shops of London, Edinburgh, Glasgow, Dublin, and other large towns, a few coming into the hands of the principal dealers every season. One caught in a stake-net near Findhorn in Scotland in July 1833, measured eight feet six inches in length, and weighed two hundred and three pounds. Pennant records the capture of one in the Esk which weighed four hundred and sixty pounds; and a head prepared by Mr. Stirling of the Anatomical Museum of the University of Edinburgh, was cut from a Sturgeon caught near Alloa, said to weigh, when entire, fifty stones, or seven hundred pounds; its length was nine feet.

The *débris* of crustaceans and half-digested pieces of fish, mixed with decaying vegetable matters and mud, have been found in the stomachs of Sturgeons, and their food is probably any soft animal or vegetable organisms that

THE COMMON BRITISH STURGEON. 13

they find at the bottom. The flesh of the Sturgeon, like that of most cartilaginous fishes, is more firm and compact than that of osseous fishes ; it generally contains much yellow fat, and is well-flavoured, easy of digestion, and very nutritious. Stewed with rich gravy, it forms a dish in high request for the table. When luxury was at its height in Imperial Rome, a Sturgeon was, according to Athenæus, the most honoured *entrée* in sumptuous repasts ; and Pliny tells us that it was crowned with flowers, and the slaves who bore it into the triclinium were also garlanded. Ovid calls it noble, either because of its costliness or of its excellence.

Tuque peregrinis Acipenser nobilis undis.

At a later period the price of a Sturgeon had fallen in Rome to four scudi, when a competition among the purveyors of the Catholic dignitaries assembled to elect a pope, in succession to Paul, produced an instantaneous rise in the market, and Cardinal Gualtheri had to pay seventy scudi for his Sturgeon. (*Richter*, Ichth.) In the time of our first Henry, the Sturgeon was reserved for the king's table, and even in the present day, when one is caught in the Thames within the jurisdiction of the Lord Mayor, it is called a Royal Fish, implying that it ought to be sent to the Queen. In Russia and other regions where Sturgeons abound, the roe dried and pressed forms the *Caviare* of commerce ; and the swimbladder treated in a particular manner furnishes highpriced isinglass.

The editor of the present edition of British Fishes has not had the advantage of personally inspecting the specimens that Mr. Yarrell had before him when he wrote his account of the Common Sturgeon, but he has seen portions of eight specimens caught in the Frith of Forth, and as such of these as have their cranial plates present a near agreement with each other in external characters, and are evidently of one species, he has drawn up an account of that species in considerable detail, adopting for it the specific appellation of *Thompsoni,* suggested by Dr. Ball. It differs in several important characters from the *Ac. sturio* of Heckel and Kner. These Frith of Forth examples agree generally with a pencil sketch sent to Mr. Yarrell by Jonathan Couch, Esq., of the cranial shields of a Sturgeon caught at Lamorna in Cornwall, in May 1851. The species, therefore, has an extensive range along the British Coasts, and may be the one to which the not very appropriate name of " Sharp-nosed " has been usually applied by English ichthyologists, though a more comprehensive comparison is needed to establish that as a fact.

Description of a Sturgeon caught in the *Frith of Forth,* and preserved in the Museum of the University of Edinburgh. Length nearly six feet. The barbels are rather nearer to the tip of the snout than to the mouth, and

THE COMMON BRITISH STURGEON. 15

when laid back do not reach the latter. They are tapering and roundish, but in the dry state show a furrow as
if they were composed of two binate cartilaginous rays.
Other Frith of Forth specimens do not exhibit this furrow. The lips, having shrunk so that their true form
cannot be ascertained, are not described. Shields or bucklers, closely connected by suture, cover the whole dorsal
aspect of the head. They are deeply pitted, the pits
being only partially disposed in rows so as to form radiating furrows. These well-defined depressions are separated by thin walls, which are crenulated, but do not rise
above the general level, so that the character of the surface is not granular. The osseous centres of most of these
shields may be made out, but they do not rise into acute
crests as in the young fish. Certain lines or ledges are
visible rather by their smoothness than by their elevation,
and the most remarkable of them present the profile of an
obelisk whose apex is in the centre of the occipital shield,
whence short lines deflect on each side to the osseous centres of the coronals. Lines proceeding from thence to the
centres of the frontals form the sides of the obelisk. Other
less conspicuous lines radiate from the same centres of
the frontals, namely, backwards over the temporals, and
forwards towards the nasal regions, with a convergence
coincident with the narrowing of the snout. The polygonal occipital shield receives the anterior point of the
first dorsal shield into a sharp mesial notch, and emits
anteriorly a salient acute process that enters between the
coronals for nearly one half of their length, these plates
coming in contact with each other for only about a third
of their length, and having the point of an interfrontal
plate insinuated between their anterior ends. This oblong interfrontal, and two other intercalary pieces, larger,
but otherwise similar to the polygonal shields which

16   ACIPENSERIDÆ.

closely cover the whole upper surface of the snout, sepa-
rate the frontals wholly from each other. The osseous
centres of the temporal shields are somewhat nearer to
the tip of the snout than those of the coronals are. On
the left side of the specimen a small squamosal interposes
between the temporal and mastoid shield, but on the other
side this piece is confluent with the temporal. A moderate inclination of the surfaces of the coronals towards
the mesial line makes a longitudinal furrow, which disap-
pears anteriorly, the interfrontal plates being nearly flat,
and the snout flatly convex transversely. Much of the
gill-flap is occupied by the large opercular shield, which
is marked by pits and furrows, with thin intervening
crenated walls distinctly radiating from a point near the
posterior edge of the plate. This shield being visible
from above merely in profile is not represented in the cut.
Behind and beneath the eye there is a rough rectangular
chevron which, in form and position, represents the preoperculum of osseous fishes. On the under surface of
the snout a raised ledge, narrow at the barbels and widen-
ing gradually in running forwards, as in the *Ac. sturio* of
Heckel, is covered either by a single slightly-rough plate,
or by several coalescent ones. The humeral plate is
deeply pitted, and the coracoid is marked by distinctly-
radiating furrows and pits.

The body-shields are radiately furrowed and pitted,
and have thin longitudinal crests. Eleven saddle-formed
shields occupy the ridge of the back before the dorsal
fin, the fourth or fifth of the series being the largest, and
the ridges of all highest in the middle. The scalene
lateral shields, lying between the suprascapular and
caudal fin, are thirty in number. In other specimens
their number varies from twenty-nine to thirty-two, there
being generally more on one side of the fish than on the

THE COMMON BRITISH STURGEON. 17

other. Heckel and Kner describe the middle lateral shields of their *Ac. sturio* as having a styloid process which proceeds forwards beneath the skin to the preceding shield, and is said to be characteristic of the species; but in the Frith of Forth Sturgeons no such process exists in any one of the whole lateral series, there being merely a notch with a flexible tube, corresponding to the lateral line of osseous fishes. There is, however, a strong and distinct smooth styloid process from the front of all the ventral shields of the Frith of Forth specimens, except the first two of the series. These ventral shields are also unequal in number, on the two sides of the fish, and vary in the specimens from nine to eleven.

The skin between the dorsal and lateral rows of shields is pretty thickly studded with star-like ossicles, intermingled with much more minute angular grains. A cluster of these ossicles is represented under the preceding wood-cut. A pair of small shields intervenes between the dorsal series and the dorsal fin, and on each side of the base of this fin there are about ten star-like ossicles larger than the others. Below the lateral shields the distinctly-stellate ossicles become fewer, and the irregular, crested grains more numerous. Between the limbs of the coracoids, and more especially a little further back below the pectorals, the skin is made rough by extremely irregular ossicles, apparently formed by the confluence of several minute angular grains and acute points, and this roughness continues onwards to the vent. The integument before the opercular shield is studded with small roundish and irregular plates, all with radiating lines from flat centres, and small plates of more oblong forms, but various outlines roughen the surface between the mouth and the coracoids.

The dorsal fin is supported by forty-one rays, the first

VOL. II. *(2nd Supp.)* F

being a flat, longitudinally-oval plate resembling the dorsal shields in size and texture, but having a small posterior peak, which rises as the first of the rays. About six stumps, seemingly bony and gradually increasing in height, follow it, and are incumbent on each other and on the flexible rays. Behind the dorsal two heart-shaped plates follow one another on the ridge of the tail. The anal, which in this specimen has been injured posteriorly, consists in others of twenty-five rays, the first being very short and incumbent, and in fact the peak of an oblong flat plate, as in the dorsal. Between this plate or fulcrum and the vent there are three pairs of small shields. An upper low caudal fin is composed of a long strap-shaped rough plate with a posterior peak, and of eighteen or nineteen firm, slender, jointless rays lying closely tiled on one another. Underneath these inflexible rays there is a triangular lateral space on each side, which is densely covered by rough, keeled, bony eminences. The under portion and main part of the caudal is lobed anteriorly, and contains numerous jointed rays. In young individuals the anterior under lobe is said not to be developed. The pectoral contains thirty-eight rays, which are prickly on the edges, and the first one is stout and bony, seemingly formed by the coalescence of about ten rays, whose number is shown by the prickly ridges which rib its surface.

Dr. James McBain, of Leith, possesses the head of a Sturgeon that was caught near Stirling, in which the cranial plates correspond almost exactly with those of the specimen described above, except that the squamosals on both sides are coalescent with the mastoidal shields. In this preparation the thin vertical plate of bone which descends from the mastoidal shield into the cranial cartilage is well shown. Dr. McBain's fish seems to have

THE COMMON BRITISH STURGEON. 19

been nearly one-third larger than the one in the Edinburgh University Museum described above.

Another perfect specimen of smaller size, being only three feet eight inches and a half long, preserved in the Museum of the Free Kirk College of Edinburgh, presents also a close similarity in the cranial plates to the two preceding, but the squamosals are both united to the temporals, and the mastoids have consequently smaller disks. In this younger fish the pits and furrows in the shields are deeper and more distinctly radiated from osseous centres. The crests of the dorsal shields are higher, and the styloid anterior processes of the ventral shields are very distinctly perceptible through the skin. The ossicles which stud the skin of the body are more generally and perfectly star-like, more of the rays being acute. There are twenty-nine lateral shields on one side, and thirty-two on the other, and the ventral shields on the right side number ten, but there are only nine on the left side. The fin-rays are—

D. 41: A. 25: P. 1 | 37: V. 27 or 28.

The osseous centres of the temporals are equidistant from the tip of the snout with those of the coronals, instead of being a little nearer, as in the other two examples, the difference being probably due to the squamosals having in this example a common centre with the temporals. The snout is also narrower, and the shields covering it are closely pressed together so as to seem confluent. This probably arises from the cartilage not having been so fully cleared out in preparation, and shrinking much in drying. To this cause also may perhaps be attributed the very slender snouts of some of the younger Sturgeons preserved in English Museums. The exact place of capture of this individual is not mentioned on the

ACIPENSERIDÆ.

label attached to it, but it has a special interest as belonging to the Museum formed by the late Professor Fleming, and, therefore, representing the *Acipenser sturio* of his British Animals.

In the Museum of the College of Surgeons of Edinburgh, there is a stuffed Sturgeon in excellent order, which measures six feet and a half in length, and does not differ materially in the form and arrangement of the cranial shields from that of the University Museum. The shields both on the head and body are, however, more deeply pitted and furrowed, their radiation is more complete, and the intervening walls of the furrows are more granulated ; more of the imbedded ossicles also are star-shaped. There are eleven dorsal shields ; thirty-two lateral ones on the left side, thirty on the right side ; and the ventral shields are ten and eleven on the right and left sides respectively. The label to this Sturgeon does not indicate its place of capture.

In the Anatomical Museum of Edinburgh University, there are preparations of several Sturgeons caught near Alloa, and in other parts of the Frith of Forth, made to exhibit the structure of the cartilaginous cranium and other internal parts. One of these shows that the occipital spine of the cartilaginous cránium is acute, and that it does not project so far back as the mastoid or par-occipital processes which are also acute. Kittary's figure of the cartilaginous cranium of his *Ac. sturio*, an inhabitant of the Caspian, represents the occiput and snout as being both widely rounded (*l. c.* Pl. vi. f. 5).

Taking Heckel and Kner as the best authorities for the continental *Ac. sturio*, and more especially for the fish of that name in the Danube, we find that, though their figures and description present many characters in common with the Frith of Forth Sturgeon, there are

THE COMMON BRITISH STURGEON. 21

some points of difference which prevent us from pronouncing on their identity without further investigation. The specific marks they assign to their *sturio* are, "premaxillary lip with an incurvature, short barbels, osseous centres of the temporals nearer to the point of the snout than those of the coronals; the process of the occipital shield that interposes between the ends of the coronals broad and chisel-shaped or truncated, and the coracoid bucklers roughly granulated, not rayed." Supposing these characters to be constant, the last-mentioned one and the truncation of the salient process of the occipital do not correspond with those parts in the British fish. The skin also of the Austrian *Sturio* is described as being studded with rough, blunt ossicles, mostly uniform in size, being merely a little larger near the head, but nowhere either radiated or stellate. In the form of the dermal ossicles the Frith of Forth Sturgeon agrees with the *Antacei* rather than with the *Sturiones*, but not with any of the six *Antacei* figured in Heckel and Kner's book. The inflexion of the upper lip belongs to all these *Antacei* except *A. schypa*.

Respecting the young, the Austrian authors so often referred to say that *Ae. sturio*, when not exceeding ten inches in length, has a stiletto-shaped snout bent upwards, the occipital enters further between the coronals; in place of the interfrontal shields there is a fontenelle, and the under anterior caudal lobe is not developed. In the Museum of the Free Kirk College at Edinburgh there is a Sturgeon, about eighteen inches long, which may probably be the young of the Frith of Forth species, described at such length in the preceding pages. It has a slender, elongated snout, evidently greatly shrunk in drying, but the arrangement of the cranial shields has much resemblance to that which exists in the older fish. The interfrontal plate is composed of six pieces, and the squamosals are not united to either the mastoids or temporals. The reason for entertaining a doubt of the identity of the species is the difference of character of the surface of both cranial and body-shields. In the small specimen the roughness of the plates is produced by round grains of various sizes disposed in radiating lines with furrows between, while in the old the crenulated edges of the thin walls that bound the depressions do not rise above the general level. The osseous centres form in the young thin crests, which on the dorsal shields have a hooked apex. A continuous crest runs from the centre of the temporal along the side of the head to that of the mastoid; and owing to the greater elevation of the centres of the coronals the mesial trough is deeper than in the larger fish, but the lines which in the latter form the profile of an obelisk are not evident. The suprascapular is pitted with radiating grooves towards its edges, and the coracoid is also decidedly radiated. The skin between the rows of body-shields is studded with roundish, irregular, very small osseous grains, the larger ones being radiated on the edges. In the recent state this radiation would be concealed by the epidermis. The barbels are short, tapering, and more remote from the tip of the snout than in larger fish. An under caudal lobe is already formed. The body-shields number fourteen on the dorsal row; thirty-eight on the right side in a line with the suprascapular, and forty on the left side; eleven ventral ones on the right side, and ten on the left. The fin-rays are—

D. 37: V. 27: A. 26.

The osseous centres of the coronals and temporals are equidistant from the tip of the snout.

The following wood-cut, reproduced from the first

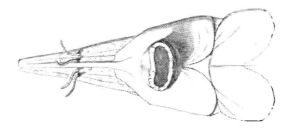

edition of British Fishes, resembles the young Sturgeon of the Free Kirk Museum in the middle ledge of the ventral aspect of the snout, not being dilated gradually towards the point, as in the larger examples. The scale is too small to give a correct idea of the form of the lips, and the figure was probably taken from a small and dried specimen.

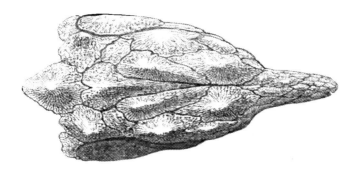

This wood-cut, which was introduced into the second edition of British Fishes, represents an arrangement of the cranial shields, differing from all the Frith of Forth examples in the want of the interfrontal plates, and in the longer tapering prolongation of the salient process of the occipital shield: the squamosals, it will be observed, are distinct pieces. The British Museum possesses a Sturgeon from Teignmouth which is four feet and three-quarters long, and another from the Thames, both with cranial shields similar to those of the cut. The barbels are short, tapering, and a little flattened, and the ossicles in the skin are partly stellate, but mostly minute and angular, as a sketch obligingly made by Mr. Gerard shows. This gentleman also mentions that the coracoid shields are netted, grooved, and radiated, and that the cranial shields are grooved and radiated with a series of ridges connecting the centres of the principal pairs of shields. If this be not a species distinct from the Frith of Forth Sturgeon it is at least a notable variety, but to be ranked equally with it among the *Antacei*, if the form of the mandibular lip will allow, and not with the *Sturiones* of Heckel and Kner. There is still needed a good description of the recent fish in various stages of its growth. This article has been extended to an unusual length, but accuracy did not seem attainable otherwise. In the terminating vignette, which appeared in the second edition of British Fishes, the intervals between the shields and the smallness of the opercular plate denote that the original was a young fish, though it does not show the thin elevated crests of the small specimen in the Free Kirk Museum.

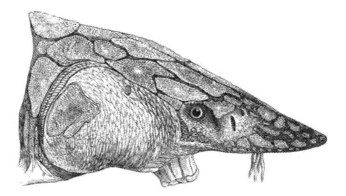

PLAGIOSTOMI.   *NOTIDANIDÆ.*
SQUALI.

THE GRAY NOTIDANUS.

Notidanus griseus, JONATHAN COUCH, Zool. for 1846, p. 1337, fig.
Hexanchus ,,   MÜLL. und HENLE, Plagiost. p. 80.
    ,,   ,,   GRAY, Cat. of Chondropt. Brit. Mus. p. 67.

NOTIDANIDÆ. *Family Characters.*—Sharks with a single dorsal and an anal fin. Head flat. A small three-cornered nasal lappet. Upper fold at the corner of the mouth very large, the under one small. Nictitating membrane wanting. Tongue adherent. Spout-holes small, perpendicular. Six or seven stigmata, diminishing successively in length, and all before the pectoral fin. A mesial tooth on the mandible: the next five or six under-teeth form a saw, by the projection of their conical cusps; the fore or inner borders of the mandibular teeth are either smooth or wholly and finely serrated; and the distal teeth of that jaw are small and flat. In the upper jaw the teeth are longer, more slender and more pointed, and their first denticle is much longer than the rest: the outer border of the upper teeth is thick, the inner one finely serrated towards its base: the foremost are hook-shaped, on a broad base, and are clustered: the next in succession have exteriorly one or two lateral denticles; and towards the corner of the mouth, the upper teeth resemble the under ones. Lateral line distinct. The single dorsal stands behind the ventrals, and partly before, partly over the anal. The caudal has small under lobes, with a notch towards the end, which is obliquely or directly docked. No caudal pits. Intestinal valve screw-shaped.

NOTIDANUS.—The only genus, subdivided by Raffinesque into *Hexanchus* and *Heptanchus*, according as the gill-openings are six or seven.

IN the year 1846 a specimen of this fish, caught by a fisherman at Polperro, was brought to Jonathan Couch, Esq., who immediately recognised it as the grey sexbranchial Notidanus, and he soon afterwards published an account of it with a figure in the Zoologist (1337).

A specimen had been also taken in the preceding year by Captain Swinburne, and presented to the British Museum, which likewise possesses a portion of the jaw from Dr. Mantell's collection. The origin of the latter is not stated, and the other two are the only instances known of this Shark being taken in the British seas.

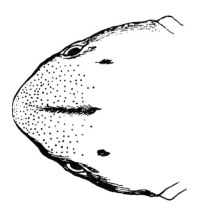

The nostril is nearer to the tip of the rounded snout than to the angle of the mouth, and the spout-hole nearer to the first gill-opening than to the eye. The hooked upper front teeth rise from a broad base, and the succeeding seven or eight large teeth are serrated on the distal edge, the first denticle being decidedly the tallest. The front mandibular tooth has lateral serratures, but no middle cusp, and the following five or six broad teeth on each side are equally serrated on the exterior and longer border by from nine to eleven denticles: their thinner inner borders are finely serrated. Dorsal notched on the edge, so placed that the anal commences before the middle of its base, and half-way between the vent and the caudal fin. Pectoral quadrangular, with rounded corners. Anal rounded anteriorly, pointed posteriorly. A distinct under lobe to the

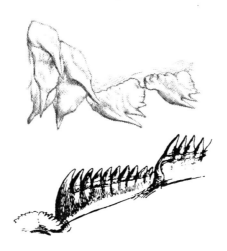

caudal with an obliquely-cut end. Scales entire and very small, leaf-shaped, with a medial keel which reaches to the acute point.—*Müller and Henle.*

Mr. Couch's specimen was two feet two inches and a half long, and was a male with small claspers. Captain Swinburne's fish was about eleven feet in length, and was captured off Ventnor in November 1845. The cuts were all drawn from this specimen.

GRAY NOTIDANUS.

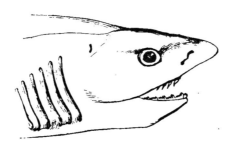

28 SCYMNIDÆ.

PLAGIOSTOMI.
SQUALI.

SCYMNIDÆ.

VALENTIN'S SEA-HOUND.

Scymnus lichia, MÜLLER und HENLE, Plagiost. 92.

SCYMNIDÆ. *Family Characters.*—Sharks having spout-holes and two dorsals without spines: no anal fin, and no nictitating membrane. Five stigmata, all of them before the pectorals. A spiral intestinal valve.

SCYMNUS. *Generic Characters.*—Head flat or laterally compressed. Spout-holes far behind and rather above the eyes. All the teeth of the upper jaw straight or vertical to the jaw, slender, hooked: the under teeth broader, with an upright or horizontal cutting edge. Stigmata small, the last two moderately approximated. No caudal pit.

In the sub-genus *Scymnus* the teeth are lancet-shaped on the mandible, sharp on the sides, tumid on the front surface, and have their lancet-shaped tips raised on an elevated base: the mesial mandibular tooth is not smaller than its neighbours, and has the basis alike on both sides, with a notch at the origin of the root. The rest of the mandibular teeth have an impress on the inner side formed by the overlying root of the next tooth. Their roots are bilobate, with a furrow. There is no prickle in the claspers.

THIS Shark occurs in Mr. Yarrell's list of new British Fishes intended for his third edition, but without any intimation of the time or place of its capture. As it is a species which inhabits the Mediterranean and the Bay of Biscay, and may be expected to enter the British Channel occasionally at least, a notice of it is given for the benefit of practical ichthyologists. The following description is quoted from Müller and Henle:—

" The nostrils are near the end of the snout, and have a small three-sided lappet on their inner border, and the hinder angle of the eye is over the corner of the mouth. Mandibular teeth serrated, fifteen in number, with two rows erected. The pectorals are round, without a hinder corner; the ventrals four-cornered and broader than the pectorals. Between the pectorals and ventrals, and rather nearer the pectorals, stands the small first dorsal, rounded, and without a hinder angle. The second dorsal is larger and four-cornered, and is situated immediately behind the ventrals; it is notched in its upper border, blunt at its fore corner, and pointed behind. Caudal fin destitute of an under lobe, three-cornered. Scales having three or more points on a four-cornered base, with three keels on the fore part. Colour violet-blackish or brownish, uniform, but with some black clouds posteriorly."

LOCH LONG, NEAR THE ENTRANCE OF LOCH GOIL.

There floated Haco's banner trim,
Above Norweyan warriors grim,
Savage of heart, and large of limb;
Threatening both continent and isle,
Bute, Arran, Cunningham, and Kyle.
                                    SCOTT.

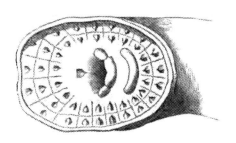

Teeth of *Petromyzon Juræ*.

The *Petromyzon Juræ*, figured in Mac Culloch's Western Isles (vol. ii. pp. 186-7, t. 29, f. 1) is probably of this genus. If the teeth are correctly represented, the fish has no relation to *Lampetra fluvialis* (vide Gray, Cat. Fish, B. Mus. p. 139). It was found adhering to a Gurnard on the coast of the island of Jura, one of the Hebrides.

END OF SECOND SUPPLEMENT
TO SECOND VOLUME.

NOTICE TO THE BINDER.

In binding the First and Second Supplements with the First Edition, place in the First Volume, after page 408 :—

The Title and Preface to the First Supplement;
The Title and Preface to the Second Supplement;
Pages 1 to 48 of the First Supplement;
Pages 1 to 36 of the Second Supplement;
The Portrait to face the Title;
The Memoir and List of Writings to follow the Title of the Work.

And in the Second Volume, after page 472, place :—
The First Supplement, pages 1 to 72;
The Second Supplement, pages 1 to 30.

In binding the Second Supplement with the Second Edition :—

The Portrait should face the Title-page;
The Memoir and List of Writings should follow the Title-page of Vol. 1;
The Title-page and Preface, and pages 1 to 36, should follow page 464 in Vol. 1.

In the Second Volume :—
Pages 1 to 30, Supplement, should follow page 628 of the Work.

N.B. The First Edition requires the two Supplements; the Second Edition requires the Second Supplement only; the third Title-page is for the convenience of those who may have already bound the First Edition in 2 vols. The two Supplements would, in this case, form the third vol.

Lightning Source UK Ltd.
Milton Keynes UK
UKOW031814060512

192143UK00006B/27/A